Life-Changing Moments in Inner Healing

Dr. Peter Mack
MBBS, FRCS, PhD

from the heart press

Publication by *From the Heart Press*:
First Publication October 2012
Website: www.fromtheheartpress.com

Copyright: Peter Mack
ISBN: 978-0-9567887-9-5

All rights reserved. Except for brief quotations in critical articles or reviews, no part of this book may be reproduced in any manner without prior written permission from the publisher.

The rights of Dr. Peter Mack as author have been asserted in accordance with the Copyright, Designs and Patents Act 1988.

A CIP catalogue record of this book is available from the British Library.

Book Artist:
Wendy Mack
Email: wendy.mzf@gmail.com

To contact the author:
Email: dr.pmack@gmail.com
Website: http://www.petermack.sg

Disclaimer

The purpose of this book is to share clinical experience. While the selected clinical vignettes describe patients with successful and dramatic outcomes, it is not the intention of the author to sensationalize hypnosis and regression therapy. Rather, the purpose is to create a wider awareness of a method of treatment that has been underutilized. No claims are made of any miraculous effectiveness of the therapy. Also, no therapists should engage in applying the powerful techniques of regression therapy unless they are adequately trained. Like other treatment, prior evaluation of a patient's suitability must be individualized on the basis of his symptoms, pathology, emotional makeup and belief system. Adequate medical opinion should always be sought before considering the treatment. No one should embark on regression therapy unless care is taken to avoid creating false memories.

Contents

Acknowledgments	vii
Preface	ix

Section A – Lady at the Window

Chapter One: Talk at the Temple	3
Chapter Two: Opening up Memories	13
Chapter Three: Flashbacks	23
Chapter Four: Karmic Debt	33
Chapter Five: Unfinished Business	49

Section B – A Call for Action

Chapter Six: Procrastination	63
Chapter Seven: Rite of Passage	75
Chapter Eight: The Archetypal Beggar	85
Chapter Nine: Rage	93

Section C – Search and Struggle

Chapter Ten: Misty Memory	107
Chapter Eleven: Fear of Success	121
Chapter Twelve: Fear of Public Speaking	129
Chapter Thirteen: Somaticized Pain	139

Section D – Scream in the Art Room

Chapter Fourteen: Snake Horror	153
Chapter Fifteen: Art and Recovery	163

Appendix: Healing & Past Life Therapy	171
Further Reading	197
Regression Therapy Associations	201
About the Author	203
Another book by the Author	205

Acknowledgments

I am grateful to my four patients, Gerald, Milton, Clarissa and Lionel (pseudonyms), who are willing to share the stories of their healing journeys with the readers and have kindly given permission to reproduce their regression experience in detail. In addition I wish to thank them for taking their time and effort to read through the manuscript to ensure factual accuracy.

I wish to thank those who have taken the trouble to read my earlier version of this book and contributed valuable suggestions for improvement. They include: Dr. Tay Sook Muay, who did her best to remain open to non-physical phenomenon while reviewing the script, Ms. Theresa Chee, whose intuitive ability has always amazed me, and Ms. Wendy Yeung, who runs a holistic healing practice.

I wish to thank my daughter Wendy, who has taken valuable time off from her studies to produce the artistic illustrations that help to bring the stories in this book alive.

Preface

This book is about *healing*. From the medical perspective the meaning of *healing* emphasizes on mending or the effecting of a cure. In contrast the holistic tradition teaches that *healing* is about regaining health at all levels and becoming wholesome with a focus not just on physical health but also on issues of personal growth, existential meaning and social organization. It brings together the mind, body and soul, and the balance between them involving the disciplines of Integrative Medicine, Psychology, Humanities and Spirituality. The term *inner healing* is used in this book to refer to the same concept and the aspects of personal wholeness sought for include love, understanding, self-awareness and soul growth. The hallmark of the process is not merely restorative but also transformational. Over and above the physical and emotional recovery, *inner healing* brings about renewal and making a comeback for the individual.

The medical professional, in the course of his career, will have encountered many challenges in managing perplexing clinical syndromes and inexplicable symptoms. In situations where Medicine has little or nothing to offer as remedy, the practitioner may sometimes heed his inner voice that calls for a search for alternatives in healing.

As health-conscious individuals most of us are taught at an early age to look after our body, but seldom are we ever taught what to do with our thoughts, feelings and emotions. When we grow up without a clear concept of who we are and believe that the physical being is all we are, we risk experiencing an incomplete self. This leads to inner stress. Beneath the attitudinal and emotional stress of many diseased patients is often a lack of a wholesome self-image. The strong capacity of the mind to combat disease and its power to restore the complete self goes unrecognized and remains encased. This book provides clinical vignettes that describe how the mind-body connection works and the extent to which the connection can be unleashed by regression therapy to overcome physical, psychological and emotional disorders.

I recall an inspiring remark made by a psychiatric colleague once: "We all know the doctor's duty is to save lives, but a higher goal is to change lives."

This book, Life-Changing Moments in Inner Healing, is about how patients' lives have been transformed. It captures the elated feelings surrounding those fateful moments during which change was initiated. The focus of the therapeutic approach in these patients is on past life regression. The idea of such a case-book was conceived soon after the publication of my previous book Healing Deep Hurt Within, which has since stirred up interest in this area among the healthcare circle.

In tracing back the memory of past life events, regression therapy exposes the issues knotted in one's inner psyche. Recalling and re-living such an experience releases the patient's inner emotional tension quickly and may provide an effective treatment option in situations where Medicine has little to contribute. The methodology is described and illustrated in detail and, where necessary, the subtle mechanisms of healing are explained. It is hoped that readers can discover through these stories the innate wisdom of their own mind-body connection and use it to enhance their own wellbeing.

Each of the four case studies has a different emotional or intra-psychic issue. The target readers are healthcare providers, therapists and patients who are in search of the meaning behind their sicknesses and the purpose of their lives. Inner psychological workings are explained at various points in the text to demystify what may otherwise appear to be a "magical" form of therapy. The underlying commonality in all four patients is their strong motivation to create change in their lives. What they lacked was external help, and I had the privilege of filling in the gap for them.

The concept of past lives will continue to remain elusive to many of us. The more technical details of the hypnotic process, trance deepening and past life exploration are included in the Appendix of this book. So are conceptual frameworks of the mind, soul and spirit. Readers with the appropriate knowledge or spiritual background will be able to connect with this last section of the book. They may be able to capture the enchanting feel of being in a past life as they immerse themselves in the mystique of the stories, even if they had not dream that they could!

Some readers may wish to regard regression therapy as another form of psychotherapy that aims at healing through persuasion. This is perfectly acceptable. The underlying assumption is that apparently "neurotic" symptoms are the external manifestations of underlying unconscious conflicts. Lifting the repression of unconscious factors and obtaining insight into the patient's core issues will resolve the symptoms and help him to heal.

Many things we encounter in our daily lives have the power to heal; be it words, touch, massage, poetry, music, crystals, art or prayers. We can also be healed by relationships, diet, exercise or medication. We can even use various aspects of our natural environment to restore our health. In hypnotherapy we commonly make use of guided imagery to help patients to achieve healing. The reader will realize that the power of healing in regression therapy resides in the recall and re-living of past events and the cathartic release of emotions that accompanies the process.

Section A

Lady at the Window

Chapter One

Talk at the Temple

> *"Much energy and ingenuity can be spent trying to prove or disprove the validity of a past life memory. Just as it's not necessary for a therapist who works with dreams to prove the scientific theory of dreams before they use it, the fact that a client seems to have a memory of a past life does not require it to be proved before working with them."*
>
> Andy Tomlinson, 2008

Stepping into a modern Buddhist temple was a memorable experience. The building was situated at the outskirts of the city, on a quiet stretch of Dunearn Road. It had no resemblance to the traditional pagoda style of architecture that I know of or have seen in my travels. In fact it did not appear externally different from any other residential mansion in the same area. As I drove into the basement car park and walked up to the courtyard, a remarkable sense of calmness and tranquility was in the air.

It was a warm Saturday afternoon. The trees and shrubs were tenderly emitting the scent of fresh chlorophyll as their leaves rustled. I felt the caress from the gentle breeze while the garden trees swayed. The path that I was walking seemed to be leading me towards to a destination that was benevolent and meaningful.

There was an unmistakable sense of serenity and wholeness in myself.

I had come in response to an invitation from a Buddhist group that was interested to learn about past life regression. I was excited. This was the first time I'd the opportunity to interact with a Buddhist audience, and I felt strange and foreign. For some years I had been delivering talks on hypnotherapy to isolated interest groups. On these occasions, nursing personnel usually formed the bulk of the audience. In all these talks I had consciously avoided the topic of past life in view of possible religious sensitivities. Matthew, a senior nursing colleague and a staunch Buddhist, had specially requested that I speak specifically on this topic at a temple venue. I jumped at the opportunity, and was upfront that I would speak from a purely intellectual perspective and in the capacity of a therapist. He quickly assured me that the audience would be comfortable with such an approach.

The sight of cleanliness in the temple and the glistening floor tiles impressed me. As I walked into the hallway, a sacred silence prevailed. The environment projected an atmosphere of soothing calm and peaceful harmony. All of a sudden, Matthew appeared in the corridor, as if he had been expecting me. He warmly introduced me to the caretaker and ushered me to the lift. He apologetically drew my attention to the poster notice next to the lift that read: "Please remove your shoes before entering the lift." I nodded in acknowledgement, followed the instruction and the lift took me to the assembly hall at the fourth level. I wondered what was awaiting me.

A warm welcome accompanied. I was again impressed. Some thirty people were already seated and more were straggling in. The assembly hall was well ventilated and brightly lit. The floor tiles appeared like glittering snow in the sunshine streaming in through the windows. At the other end of the hall was a statue of Gautama

Buddha, approximately two and half times life-sized. It was sculptured from white marble, mounted behind glass panels and installed centrally against the wall. Unlike traditional Buddhist temples, there were no joss sticks, joss papers, candle-holders, nor any smell of incense that typically permeates a prayerful environment. Instead, on either sides of the statue were drop-down projection screens ready for PowerPoint slide projection. I realized they were all prepared for my talk.

I halted for a moment and quietly focused my visual attention on the awesome statue in respectful silence. It was a privilege to address a group of spiritual followers in the sacred presence of the Buddha himself, I thought. Mostly young and middle-aged people, the audience were quietly seated on the floor on dark brown cushions, most of them being in the lotus position as if ready to meditate.

It was a big hall and I was provided with a wireless microphone. With the Buddha statue behind me and the solemn silence of the audience in front, it felt as if I was about to deliver a sermon rather than a lecture. Suddenly, deep within I had an intuitive sense that I was about to step into the transformational path of someone's life ...

I began my talk with an introduction of the concept of hypnosis, the creation of trance states, use of visualization and the healing power that could be harnessed from hypnotic suggestions and guided imagery. Next I explained the mind-body-soul connection and how a patient under hypnosis could be guided into one of his previous lives. I dealt with the mechanisms of healing and the theory of the soul journey, explaining how past life memories could influence who we are in the present life. Following that I elaborated on how eliciting past life memories provides the platform for the therapist and client to re-work the stories of past life trauma together to obtain rapid healing for the patient. I concluded with a few illustrative case stories.

The talk at the Buddhist temple ended on a very positive note. As a significant part of the subject matter was technical, I have appended most of the content of the talk at the back of this book for the interested reader.

A rush of excitement followed as I concluded my talk, following which several members of the audience came forward. Many were interested to know in greater depth about the subject while others continued to ask questions to clarify the extent of healing possibilities. Twenty minutes later the crowd adjourned to a tea reception in the dining hall one level below and we continued to share viewpoints.

What was unknown to me at that point in time was that Gerald, who had sat quietly at the back of the assembly hall, had badly wanted to meet me. For years he had been troubled by a complex personal issue associated with occasions of déjà vu [1] experiences. Not getting an opportunity because of the crowd, he decided to leave quietly with his wife with the intention of looking me up on a future occasion.

Gerald was a bright young man in his thirties. A month after the event at the temple, he got in touch with me through his wife, Sarah, who happened to work as a hospital administrator.

One day, Sarah asked me timidly if I would mind looking into her husband's problem.

"Sure," I responded. "But what is his issue?"

"Several," she replied, "including insomnia, nightmares, strange dreams, unexplained visions, water phobia, emotional tiredness, etc."

Gerald was known to have congenital heart disease and from young had been unfavorably perceived as a sick child by his

---

[1] The term "déjà vu" is French and refers to an overwhelming sense of familiarity

parents. The hole-in-the-heart had since closed in his adulthood. His biggest problem was that he had not been sleeping well for many years.

As a child Gerald experienced bad dreams almost nightly. The dreams were repetitive in theme. Typically he would dream of himself running away fearfully from an unseen enemy. At other times he would dream of himself running frantically up and down a staircase. When he woke up in the mornings, he felt emotionally tired. Added to this he had recently been experiencing spontaneous visions of himself enclosed behind bars in an unknown prison. This made him very anxious and worried.

From the medical perspective, dreaming is a form of sleep thinking, but in the form of visual-motor imagery rather than words. Psychologically, dreams are understood to represent intra-psychic conflicts, and these conflicts often involve interpersonal relationships that are important to the dreamer. Sigmund Freud considered dreams as the *royal road to the unconscious*, and I personally felt this to be true in my hypnotherapy practice.

Intrigued with Gerald's story, I immediately agreed to help him to explore his problem. We met for the first time on 24 September 2011, and that turned out to be an unforgettable day in Gerald's life.

Gerald had a longish face with a sharp chin, with deep-set brown eyes that carried with them an intriguing inscrutability. He had a simple, no-fuss hairstyle. His hair was short at the back and around the sides with the top hair layer cut clipper-short and getting gradually longer at the front. His self-introductory story was short, crisp and amazing.

Gerald's mother died when he was only nine years old. After that he went through the unpleasantness of having to deal with the bullying behavior of his close childhood friends. He strongly felt they had betrayed his trust. Next he recalled vivid memories of a *near-death experience* at the age of around twelve to thirteen years.

"What actually happened at that time?" I asked curiously.

"I was told that my heart stopped for no reason," he said. "I was sleeping at home one day and my father tried to wake me up and couldn't," he said. Then his father rushed him to hospital in an ambulance, following which he went through a most memorable experience.

I listened with excitement.

"That night, my mum came to see me ..." he mumbled. His eyes appeared misty and it sounded as if his feelings were getting mixed up.

"My dad had wanted to get another mum for me. I am the youngest in the family. I am also the one who is most problematic, such as my hole-in-the-heart and a lot of other illnesses. Hence my mum wanted to bring me along with her," he said with a sad tone.

"It was as if I had a strange *dream*,' he talked softly. "I saw myself lying on my bed. I woke up and turned around to look at myself. I didn't know why I did so, but I saw myself still lying on the bed." His eyes were dreamy, like dim skies.

I had previously encountered people who had come close to death, and went through a profound experience in which they seemed to leave their physical body and enter some other realm that transcended their ego and the confines of time and space. This has been termed *near-death experience* or NDE for short. Gerald had read a lot about similar stories and felt that his own experience was very similar.

"Were you surprised at seeing yourself then?" I asked.

"No, I wasn't surprised and I didn't feel afraid because I thought it was just a dream," he replied firmly.

He recalled how he slowly stepped out of bed, leaving his physical body behind, and stood up on the floor. Next he saw a door in front of him. He wanted to leave the room and walked slowly towards it. On reaching the door he realized it was locked.

"So I tried to open the door, and when I could not open it, I just walked through the door," he said without too much emotion.

"What? You mean you walked right through?" I was fascinated.

In the past I had interviewed people who had gone through NDE, and I continued to be intrigued by each and every story that I captured. Consistently the individual would recount an ineffable experience that included feelings of peace and calm, being out of the physical body and movement through a special path. Frequently the path described was that of a tunnel and with a light at the other end. There might be a meeting with other spiritual beings and the individual would eventually arrive at a border of no return before returning to the physical body. Of note, the experience would often be accompanied by profound changes in attitudes, beliefs and values upon coming out of the experience. Then signs of accompanying spiritual growth would often become visible. I realized subsequently that this was also the case with Gerald.

"Yes, I could really walk past the door and through it to the balcony," Gerald said. "I walked through it because I couldn't open the door. When I walked through the door I felt electrified ... as though there was a lot of static electricity around me. I felt as if an electric current passed through my body."

There was a shiver in Gerald's body as he described that memorable moment.

"My mother was outside the building waiting for me with her male friend from the other world. They were in a car. So I just opened the car door and popped into it. The next thing I experienced ... *everything was white.*"

The last three words struck a chord. I had on several occasions encountered an identical expression in my regression practice. In the context of spirituality, the *white light* is representative of the energy of the *Higher Self*. Not infrequently, the light is of a blinding nature and yet feels like a peaceful aura. I have been taught that the way for the departed soul to travel to the soul plane to select its own future is to enter this white light. In this instance, Gerald had stopped short of entering the white light.

"I saw my mum," he continued. "She was dead but I saw her and her male friend from the other world. After I boarded their car I experienced a floating feeling while sitting inside. It seemed as if my mum and her boyfriend had wanted to bring me to somewhere, but then again the two of them didn't talk.

"The next thing I saw was this big ... very big door. It was a wooden gate, red in color. It looked like an ancient Tang Dynasty gate. I tried to push it but couldn't open it. Then I suddenly woke up. I believe it was not time for me to go yet." Gerald ended the story with a sad tone.

NDE is currently being used as evidence for the existence of the soul. Scientists have offered physiological explanations for NDE on the grounds that the temporal lobe of the brain may respond to the oxygen lack by generating strong emotions as the heart stops. However, studies of hypoxic (oxygen lack) experiences from mountain trackers and pilots have shown that lack of oxygen produces increasing confusion instead. The confusion is then followed by a loss of perception before lapsing into the unconscious state. This is inconsistent with the vividness of the experience during NDE. Skeptics have also argued that because consistent reports of NDEs have gained widespread exposure, people are conditioned to have them. However, this did not sound plausible in Gerald's case.

Ever since his NDE, Gerald had become more intuitive and began to experience spontaneous visions in his day-to-day life. His visions were always on the same theme and appeared enigmatic. Each time he could make out a face at the window – the facial appearance of a young lady with long hair, expressionless and standing by the window as if she had a message for him. Yet, she never talked and Gerald did not know her identity. However, at times he seemed to be able to communicate with her telepathically to a certain extent. Intuitively he felt connected to this lady at a deeper level and in some unknown manner. The same face had kept appearing in his dreams until he was sixteen years of age. He remained very puzzled with the vision.

As a rule Gerald's dreams were both realistic and vivid. They were invariably associated with the déjà vu feeling of half-conscious memories. As he grew older, the dream content changed. He would experience himself running desperately away from someone, as if he was being predated upon. At other times, he felt that he was chasing somebody. In more recent times, he began to see himself imprisoned behind metal bars. The frustration was that he was unable to find an explanation for any of these dreams, though at a deeper level he felt a unifying reason underlying these phenomena. On all these occasions, "normal" dream features were absent. There were no familiar people, places, symbols nor archetypes. This led me to suspect his dreams were past life dreams. I had learned from my training that past life dreams tend to appear at a critical time in one's life when the *collective unconscious*[2] opens to give the individual guidance. Past life dreams are meant to serve as a reminder to the individual as to what he has been through before.

Gerald was also aware of an irrational fear of water from a very young age. He recalled one instance in which he was swimming in his grandfather's *kelong*[3] in the Punggol area and was

---

[2] Collective unconscious is a term in analytic psychology coined by Carl Jung. It refers to that part of the unconscious mind that is of a universal and impersonal nature and which is identical in all individuals. It consists of pre-existing archetypes that give forms to certain psychic content.

[3] The word *kelong* is Malay in origin and describes an offshore fishing platform and a unique fishing strategy devised by early Southeast Asian fishermen.

nearly drowned by accident. The nightmarish experience had greatly intensified his hydrophobia since.

In addition, he had an unexplainable sense of hatred of betrayal. He hated organizational backstabbing and had wanted badly to leave his current job. Several of his corporate colleagues had let him down and betrayed his trust. On the other hand, he hesitated because Sarah had been upset and felt insecure with his intention to resign.

Gerald's story kept me spellbound, like a child to whom the nurse is telling some wonderful story. Towards the end, I concluded that Gerald was likely to find answers to his issues through a past life regression.

Chapter Two

Opening up Memories

"When you begin to open up the memories of your past lives, you most often remember first the emotions contained within the memory, rather than the event that originated the emotions. This is because your memories are filled by your feelings. You may see a brief image or fragment of a past life memory that will cause the associated emotions to surface. A past life memory may be triggered by a present situation that is similar to a past experience, and you may find yourself responding to the emotions from your past life memory without recalling the details of the corresponding memory. This can help you to understand situations where your feelings are out of context with the present situation."

Gloria Chadwick

It was mid-afternoon. Dressed in a collarless T-shirt, Gerald had comfortably positioned himself on a reclining chair and was covered with a blanket. He was all ready for a past life regression. I inserted a CD into a player and allowed the soft and low-toned meditation music to fill the room for a couple of minutes to prime the session. Meditation music instills peace and helps the listener to acquire a sense of discovery.

"Take a deep breath slowly, concentrating on the air entering your chest," I said.

Almost all relaxation techniques start with deep breathing. It is a simple yet powerful relaxation technique providing a quick way to get one's stress level in check.

"Feel the relaxation entering your body as you inhale to your fullest ... and as you breathe out feel the tension leaving your body."

After taking three deep breaths Gerald was visibly relaxed. The low bass tones and the whooshing sound of the music had a trance-like quality and helped him rapidly to reach a state of calm.

Next I directed his attention to the top of his head. "Feel the scalp muscle relaxation descending on both sides of your temples, your forehead, face and right down to the lips. Make sure your teeth are not clenched and let your jaw hang loosely ... now you will find that your whole head is relaxed."

I next guided the relaxation down the neck, shoulders, upper limbs, chest and the paraspinal muscles all the way down to the lower lumbar spine. Next I gave another set of suggestions to relax the lower half of the body, the pelvis, buttocks, hips, groins, thighs, knees and all the way down to the ankles, feet and toes. The principle behind the use of progressive muscle relaxation in hypnotic induction is that whatever relaxes one's muscles will also relax one's mind. Relaxing each muscle group at a time until the entire body is relaxed leads to an effective calming of the mind.

During the mid-stage of the induction I noticed a sudden, brief jerk of the body, and I made a point to check it out with Gerald during the post-therapy debrief. He recalled experiencing himself being "electrified" at that point when he was entering a trance state.

Six minutes passed. I noticed some flickering of Gerald's eyelashes. His breathing had slowed down and became more regular. He seemed to be in a hypnotic state. I checked his hypnotic depth with the eye-catalepsy and arm-catalepsy tests. Then I proceeded to deepen his trance using a visual imagery of himself walking slowly down a flight of stairs.

By now fifteen minutes had elapsed. Gerald was visualizing himself at the bottom of the staircase and the moment had come to guide his entry into a past life.

"You see a door in front of you," I suggested, and he affirmed it with an ideomotor signal[4] from his finger. "Walk slowly towards it. As you are getting closer ... put your hand on the handle ... open it wide and step into a garden. Look around. It is a beautiful garden ... you see flowers, trees and shrubs. Walking through the garden will eventually lead you to a past life that is related to this lady at the window whom you have been envisioning.

"As you continue to walk you see a mist building up in front of you. It is slowly becoming thicker. Walk towards it because you know that this mist is the doorway to your past life. In a moment you are stepping into it. One ... you walk right into the mist and the cloud-like aggregate is slowly coming around you by your side. Two ... you walk further into the middle of the mist and everything gets blurred. You find yourself surrounded by a hazy environment and you know you are one step nearer to your past life. Three ... as you walk out of the mist into your past life, you find the vision in front of you clearing up."

The past life story emerged.

"A street ..." Gerald said softly. "It's daytime. I am a man about twenty years of age, wearing a singlet and slippers on my feet. My surname is Chang."

"What are you doing now?"

"I am standing. People around me are buying drinks from me."

"What drinks are they buying from you?" I asked.

"Soft drinks with ice water," he mumbled. It sounded like a scene in a hawker stall.

---

[4] Ideomotor signaling is a psychological phenomenon when an individual makes a motion unconsciously with his finger in response to the therapist's question.

"What is this place that you are in?" I asked further.

There was a sense of hesitation as Gerald paused to embody himself in the past life scene. "It looks like Chinatown," he replied.

Things began to make sense. Chinatown is an old part of Singapore City with distinctly Chinese cultural elements. It is also a neighborhood with a historically concentrated ethnic Chinese population. Large sections of it have been declared national heritage and many buildings have been preserved in their original form to this day. Seemingly, in his past life Gerald was a hawker selling drinks from a roadside stall. The use of hawker carts was a common sight in the old days.

"Look at the people around you. Is anyone talking to you?"

"No ..." he replied.

There was a sense of anxiety in his voice. A period of silence followed. I waited. Forty seconds elapsed and at the next statement, the story seemed to be taking shape.

"An old lady, about fifty years of age ... she has fallen down the stairs."

"What happened after she fell?"

"She's bleeding from the head ... and crying. I am running towards her ... Her daughter has been taken away by the Japanese soldiers. Her daughter is in her twenties. I cannot catch up with them." Gerald sounded anxious, but remained in trance.

Immediately I became alert. The story sounded like a familiar and frightening account of painful memories of the Japanese Occupation in Singapore during World War II.

"Do you know the daughter?"

"Yes. Her mother wants us to get married."

As the story evolved, Gerald's intention was to run after the Japanese soldiers to rescue the daughter, but was promptly stopped by someone.

"A man appears ... he is my friend. He stops me."

The man referred to was subsequently identified by the name Ah Seng, his childhood friend in that past life. Ah Seng owned an adjacent roadside cart-hawker store to Gerald's selling cooked noodles.

Gerald had no idea why he was stopped at that point in time, but it seemed that Ah Seng had his safety at heart. As a matter of fact, he reminded Gerald to give priority to attending the old lady's injury.

"He [Ah Seng] takes the old lady to a *sinseh*[5] ... the bleeding doesn't stop. The old lady gives me a piece of red colored paper with her daughter's name, birth date and birth time written on it. She asks me to save her daughter from the Japanese soldiers, and to marry her after that. I agree to her request and tell her not to worry."

Traditional Chinese culture requires the child's birth data to be documented on a red piece of paper, the red color being symbolic of luck. Such data were meant for calculating the *Eight Characters* or deriving the *Four Pillars of Destiny*. The latter is used for compatibility analysis prior to matchmaking or marriage in the same way as synastry is practiced in Western Astrology.

After a minute of silence, Gerald jumped to an earlier scene of his past life. In regression practice, this phenomenon of non-sequential recall is quite common and seldom ever creates a problem for the therapist.

"It is a busy street. I am selling drinks. Ah Seng is selling noodles. We are both hawkers. A pretty lady, Mei Fung, eighteen years of age, comes along to buy drinks. She always buys Royal Crown." Apparently Mei Fung came from Trengganu, Malaysia and moved to Singapore with her mother in search of a better job.

---

[5] *Sinseh* is a term in the local vernacular and refers to a practitioner of traditional Chinese Medicine.

"She is the one taken away by the Japanese. We are dating ... I see a lot of Caucasians ... We are at the funfair. Ah Seng plays *tikam–tikam*[6] and wins five dollars as third prize in the game.

"Ah Seng has bought a lot of things with the money ... roast duck ... satay ... for Mei Fung's mother. We're going home. Ah Seng and I are cycling. Mei Fung is sitting behind me." There was a faint smile on Gerald's expression as he was describing the scene, but this soon faded as a more serious tone took over.

"Ah Seng has something to tell me. He wants to bring me to somewhere. He brings me to the hut, the one in the forest. He introduced me to the group. He tells me that he is in the guerilla group. I accept their invitation to join the group. Mei Fung does not know that I am part of the group.

"I see a wooden hut ... a forest ... with the men. There are about ten of us inside the hut, all men. There is a wooden crate ... rifles ... weapons. The Japanese are not here yet. They are still in Nanjing. I am in charge of ammunition. We are using Mark II rifles ..."

"What happens next?"

"We arm ourselves ... to fight the Japanese. A map ... Ah Seng takes out a map ... (pause). It's a river at Punggol. He tells us about a *kelong*."

Gerald had spent his childhood in a coastal area called Punggol, situated in northeastern Singapore. His late grandfather used to own a *kelong* but that had since been demolished.

"The *kelong* looks familiar ... The Japanese soldiers are coming in a *sampan*[7] ..." he said excitedly.

---

[6] The word *tikam* comes from the Malay language meaning "random pick". In the old days, it described a simple game where people get to pick random numbered tickets and have a chance to win a prize.

[7] A *sampan* is a flat-bottomed Chinese boat approximately 3.5 to 4.5 meters in length, used as a traditional fishing boat. It is either propelled by oars or fitted with an outboard motor.

"They are beating up a young man. They take his fish and leave ... Oh! The *kelong* looks like my grandfather's *kelong* ... and the young man looks like my grandfather!" A tone of surprise sounded in his voice.

The story suddenly came to a standstill. I waited and then decided to direct Gerald to another significant event.

"A forest ... there's gunfire ... an ambush. We've ambushed the Japanese."

The story gathered momentum again.

"Ah Seng has been hit ... I drag him to behind a wooden log ... Oh dear! He is going to die. I try to carry him ..." A sad expression showed up on his face.

"What happened next?"

"A prison ... metal bars. I'm in prison ..."

At this point I was immediately reminded of Gerald's recent vision of himself behind bars.

"An officer appears ... He's bald ... talking in Japanese. He drags me to an open field under the sun." Gerald's voice lowered and his breathing suddenly turned heavy.

"Ouch, ouch ... ooouch ..." Gerald cried in pain. Furrows appeared on his forehead. With his eyes still closed, his eyelid muscles tensed up. The skin of the center of his forehead was pulled down to between the eyebrows. The upper lips became elevated and the nasal wings were stretch. At the same time, the corners of the mouth were pulled sideways, raising the cheeks and partly exposing the upper row of teeth. For about two minutes, he was grimacing with pain and there were short gasps of heavy breathing.

"What is happening?"

"He's slashed me with his sword. It is painful at the abdomen." Gerald was in agony. A tear-drop rolled down the left cheek. He sniffed his nose and continued: "He has cut me all over." He was referring to a Japanese officer who held a samurai sword.

"What happened next?"

"Back to the cell ... I am bleeding ... Torture! They are trying to drown me by force in a wooden bucket of water!"

I shuddered like a sick patient in fever myself. At this stage I recalled some of the horror stories of the use of torture tactics on World War II captives that I have heard as a child.

"They show me a picture of Lim Bo Seng, and ask if I know him. When I say 'I don't' they keep dunking my head under water repeatedly."

It sounded ghastly. There was a deep anger in Gerald's voice. The psychic origin of his water phobia now became obvious.

From what I remembered from history studies in my early schooldays, Lim Bo Seng was a national hero of Singapore and was well known for his resistance to the Japanese forces during World War II. When the Japanese launched their full-scale operation in Singapore and Malaysia to destroy the spy network, they went to the extent of torturing all captured prisoners to extract clues of his whereabouts.

The life of Lim Bo Seng rapidly flashed through my mind. A native Chinese, he moved to Singapore at the age of sixteen and inherited his father's business four years later. When the second Sino-Japanese War broke out in 1937 he raised funds to help China fight the Japanese invasion. In 1938 he went to Malaysia to lead a tin-mine workers' strike against the Japanese. In 1941 he was in charge of organizing a group of volunteer fighters. In 1942 when the Japanese captured Singapore he fled to India to join a resistance force organized by the British. This was the year that Gerald's past life story took place.

By then I realized Gerald had remained silent for several moments. "What happened next?" I asked.

"Oh ...!" He suddenly cried in pain again. "They've hammered my finger ... they are laughing." I noted tears were beginning to form in his eyes, and he started to sniff again as his sinuses turned wet.

"Where are you now?"

"I am in a truck ... they are bringing me to some place ... I am blindfolded ... with many others on the truck."

"Where do they intend to bring you?"

"No idea." There was a pause.

"Go to the point where the truck dropped you. What did you experience?"

"Waves ... I hear the sound of waves. I am blindfolded still. My bare feet are feeling the heat of the hot sand on the beach. I am now in a kneeling position. There are many of us. We're at the seaside. They are going to execute us ..." Gerald's breathing turned deep and heavy again and he sounded very frightened.

"They are cocking their weapons." The fear in his voice rose to a crescendo.

"They are talking in Japanese language ... Someone is giving an order ... They open fire ... we are being shot." Gerald tensed up for a moment and then his voice slowly softened.

"What happened to you?"

"I am lying down on the sand in pain. I am hit ... I feel numb ... feel cold ... can't breathe. I'm choked ... I don't feel anything ... I feel nothing ... I am choked ... I am breathless."

Tension was rapidly leaving Gerald's body and all his muscles were visibly relaxed.

"And what happened next?"

Later I was told that Gerald was feeling the departure of his soul from the body at this point. He began to experience things differently then.

"White ... Everything is white. I see myself on the beach. I am standing up ... looking at all the bodies, including my own. I have completely left my body. I feel relaxed ... Everything is white."

His repeated utterance of the white color reminded me of his out-of-body experience.

"Tell me what happened next?"

There was a long pause.

"Hospital bed ... I see a lady in a hospital bed ... she is smiling at me. She's crying ... She tells me that she's waiting for me. She's the same girl who was taken away by the Japanese."

"Are you dead or alive at this point?"

"We are both dead ... (pause). She tells me how she died. She was raped ... she bit her tongue and committed suicide. I did not manage to see her after she was taken away by the Japanese," he said, sounding very remorseful.

One hour and twenty minutes elapsed and I ended the session by bringing Gerald out of hypnosis with a simple backward countdown of five to one. The moment Gerald was fully round, he felt very, very tired. He recalled being in deep trance throughout, and was barely aware of what was going on.

I too felt tired. The past life story had not emerged in sequence. Nonetheless the session provided me with enough information to understand the karmic origin of Gerald's symptoms.

Chapter Three

Flashbacks

"We all have traumas from the past that affected us so strongly that we continued for years to respond to that trauma through our attitudes, expectations and feelings about ourselves, others, and our environment. We cannot take away our memories of what happened, but we can release the trauma, misunderstandings and negative expectancies associated with those memories. Thus we reintegrate the memories, creating new associations and feelings. We can transform the relevance of the experience to our lives."

Randall Churchill, 2002

Healing seemed to have set in immediately. For the first time in fifteen years, Gerald enjoyed the comfort of a dream-free sleep that night.

In the evening after the therapy session Gerald decided to relax himself and join his friends for a group gathering. It was a wonderful supper party in which he could catch up with his former colleagues. He enjoyed some lovely seafood and felt really good after a hearty conversation with the group. He came home late, at around 11 pm, to take a shower. Just when he was beginning his shower, something unexpected happened ...

As the water from the shower head accidentally splashed onto Gerald's face, wetting his nose and mouth, it suddenly triggered a flashback of the past life scenes visualized earlier in the day. The water dripping onto his nose and mouth had "reminded" him of his imprisonment during the Japanese Occupation when his head was forcibly dunked under water to extract a confession. The unconscious mind seemed to work efficiently with analogies!

It was around midnight when Gerald finished the shower. He sat down quietly, closed his eyes and relaxed into a reclining sofa. Within moments, he entered a trance state unaided. Then he started telling Sarah that he could visualize all the past life scenes that he experienced earlier in the day, some of which he had failed to visualize earlier. While still in trance, he started talking. Suddenly Sarah realized that he was re-experiencing and reiterating his past life story all over again, and unaided by the therapist! Alerted, she immediately took out her iPhone and documented all she heard.

After the flashbacks were over, Gerald realized he could actually recall most of his past life story on his own. With a sigh of satisfaction, he felt more peaceful now and decided to go to bed.

That night proved to be a wonderful change for Gerald. The fear and tension of facing bad dreams had somehow vanished … like a burst bubble! For the first time he was free from worries and enjoyed a deeply relaxed and peaceful sleep. He woke up fresh the next morning and wrote: "Last night I had no dreams. That is the first time that I have got no dreams, but images just keep on coming now and then." He was referring to his spontaneous flashbacks that intermittently presented themselves.

Next day, Sarah showed me her transcript of what Gerald had uttered under trance the night before. To my pleasant surprise, the content was identical to what Gerald had said to me during the regression process! Like most patients undergoing treatment, he had been bravely confronting the intense emotions released when the traumatic past life memories surfaced during the session. This was a significant step in his healing. Rather than rationalizing the emotions away, he was making an effort to come to terms with them. In this respect, I was keen to get more information on the images of the spontaneous flashbacks that he continued to experience.

In the afternoon, Gerald was driving from his home in the new Punggol estate to the city via the Tampines Expressway. However, he was vulnerable to *highway hypnosis*[8] and had to actively manage the mental images that kept intruding into his consciousness. As he continued to experience flashbacks, Sarah became very worried and tried distracting him to make him concentrate on the driving.

Eventually Sarah gave me an update on her husband's flashbacks. Interestingly, four sets of images were identified:

Image Set 1: A rubber plantation
"I saw a rubber plantation. This plantation is appearing in night time because I saw the candle lighted on the trees. I know it is a rubber tree because I saw the tapped marks on the trunk." Somehow the image of the rubber plantation was surfacing repeatedly and he had no idea how it could be linked to his past life.

Image Set 2: An island
"The next image I saw was the beach. It was day time. I saw an island opposite the beach. It was a relatively small island with few coconut trees. It was very near to the shore of the beach ... maybe only a few hundred meters away." Apparently this was the same beach close to where his grandfather's *kelong* used to be erected. Furthermore, the image of the island continued to appear in subsequent regressions.

Image Set 3: A prison
"My flashbacks indicate a cell with high ceiling ... white and blue colored walls. It should be a colonial-era building in view of such a high ceiling ... the lamp, the switches, the clock and the wooden chair." This was the place where he saw himself behind bars.

---

[8] *Highway hypnosis* is a phenomenon of driving without attention. A person goes into a dreamy state while driving a vehicle on a long, monotonous highway, and has to grapple with a mental duality, with one stream of consciousness focused on driving and another stream apparently focused on elsewhere.

Image Set 4: A street in Chinatown
"I keep on seeing that street where I used to sell drinks. It is a curved street, lined by shop houses. The other hawkers are selling noodles. It is a street within a Chinese community for sure. It is such a narrow street that only one car of modern-day size can pass through. Alongside these images is a sense of *unfinished business*," Gerald said.

Fig. 1: "A curved street – where I used to sell drinks."

I was alerted to his use of the term *"unfinished business"*. I understood that to mean feelings that were not integrated or unresolved emotions that were connected to his past life. I was a little concerned because such residual emotions were likely to continue to impact his emotional functioning.

Over the next fortnight, Gerald continued to experience dream-free sleep. However, on 12 October Sarah informed me that he had started to experience some abdominal pains. "It was as if his tummy had been slashed by a knife," she said. This put me on the alert. The spillover emotions from the past life trauma of being tortured by Japanese soldiers seemed to have had a somaticizing[9] effect. I asked Sarah if he would like to come back for therapy. Unfortunately, he was not available then, because of work commitments.

On 22 October Sarah called me to say that Gerald had had dreams about Japanese soldiers chasing him again. This had been going on for the few previous nights. "He held my hands before he slept while I was still awake, and within moments his body started to twitch," Sarah said with a worried tone. "A minute or so later, when he was more alert, I asked him if he'd had nightmares. His reply was: 'Japanese soldiers are chasing after me and I am running'. Then he went back to sleep."

That night Gerald experienced flashback of the Japanese soldiers again, but it was a more ghastly scene this time. He saw a meter-long wooden bench positioned on the street outside the *kempeitai*[10] headquarters, and the location seemed to be Eu Tong Sen Street. Three decapitated heads were placed on the bench with blood dripping down onto the ground!

This was dumbfounding. It also provided a fresh insight. I inferred that there were probably more details in the past life story waiting to be elicited. Sarah was getting increasingly concerned. I asked if Gerald could possibly document his visual images in drawing. He was reluctant and gave his lack of artistic skills as the excuse. Then he changed his mind after Sarah's persuasion.

---

[9] *Somaticization* is the unconscious channeling of repressed emotions into somatic, or bodily symptoms. In psychodynamic theory this phenomenon is conceptualized as a mechanism of ego defense.

[10] The *kempeitai* was the military police arm of the Japanese Imperial Army during the Japanese occupation. It came under the jurisdiction of the Ministry of War in Japan. It was led by Lieutenant Colonel Oishi Masayuki with headquarters in the old YMCA in Singapore.

Fig. 2: Gerald's sketches of some of his flashback scenes

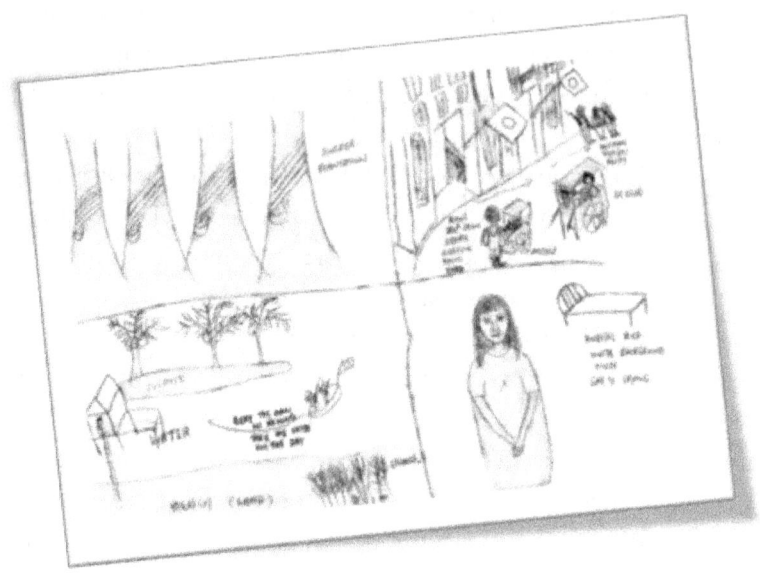

He took a sheet of A4 paper, divided it up into four quadrants with a pencil cross and started drawing. On the left upper quadrant he sketched the outline of four trees with oblique grooves and hanging cups. This represented the rubber plantation that had been appearing in his flashbacks. As yet, he was not able to tell me the significance of these rubber trees.

On the right upper quadrant, he drew a panoramic view of a row of old shop houses in a street in Chinatown. There were Japanese flags hanging out of the shop windows. A woman had fallen down the staircase with bleeding from the scalp. Two Japanese soldiers had arrested a girl and were dragging her away. On the street were two mobile hawker carts. On one cart was Gerald himself selling bottled and iced-drinks and on the adjacent cart was Ah Seng selling cooked noodles. This was exactly like he had described during his regression experience. As yet he was still unaware of the name of the street where the event took place.

On the lower left quadrant he sketched his grandfather's *kelong* and two Japanese soldiers coming in a sampan. The soldiers had robbed his grandfather of his catch while Gerald was hiding behind the forest spying on the Japanese. On the opposite shore was an island with coconut trees that he had been envisioning. Again, he was unable to tell me the whereabouts of this island.

On the right lower quadrant he sketched a simple portrait of Mei Fung and the hospital bed on which he saw her lying. Upon completion, he felt satisfied and amazed at how much the simple drawing resembled her appearance.

Very soon, he experienced the impact of an unexplained anxiety which had been building up while he was drawing. By the time Gerald had finished all the sketches, he started to experience a mounting fear. Bit by bit, he began to recall the frightening details of the past life memories again ...

I received a frantic phone call from Sarah at around 11 pm. There was a panicky voice at the other end of the line. According to her, Gerald's fear had continued to mount after completing the drawings, and had since escalated out of proportion. Once again he had slipped into trance and self-regressed.

Back into the same past life, he started getting flashbacks, scene by scene, of all the horrifying moments when he was tortured by the Japanese soldiers. He described in detail how he ran away from the Japanese soldier who eventually caught him and tortured him in jail. He recalled his body being thrown into the sea after he was shot dead. By then he didn't even dare to wash his face because of his fear of water.

Gerald appeared delirious, which was when Sarah rang me and quickly described what was happening. I felt that Gerald needed prompt assistance to quiet him down.

My mind worked quickly. I recalled that Sarah had been a Yoga student and had learned relaxation techniques in her classes. I suggested that she immediately give instructions to Gerald on deep breathing exercises.

The strategy worked!

Sarah heaved a sigh of relief as Gerald's agitated state mellowed with each deep breath that he took. It was 11:40 pm. Gerald had just emerged successfully from his trance state. He had calmed down and felt a little tired. He wanted to go to sleep. Gerald and Sarah were both in their bedroom. Alas ... something happened again.

Fig. 3: "I stepped into a different dimension upon clicking the switch!"

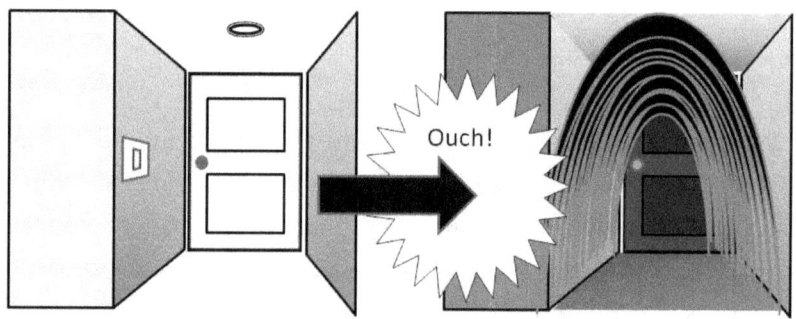

The entrance door to their bedroom was at the end of a short passageway. Thinking that he would retire to bed, Gerald walked towards the door, and on the way pressed the wall switch to turn off the ceiling lights. As the room darkened he continued with his next few steps on the way to the door, and suddenly experienced a transformation of the environment around him. It was a shocking experience. The perception was that he was walking in a "dark tunnel", like having stepped into a "different dimension".

As he reached the far end of the "tunnel", he turned the door lock and heard the "click" of the locking mechanism. It was a memorable moment. At the sound of the click, he started spiraling into a trance state once more. Slowly, he turned round and walked back towards his bed while still in trance.

At that instant, flashbacks of the past life scenes occurred again. He saw himself revisiting the same gory scene of the three decapitated heads lying on a wooden bench. Blood was seen dripping from the bench onto the floor. It was ghastly! Then he saw himself back in the same old Eu Tong Sen Street and recognized the characteristic high walls of the shop houses. Fear gripped him!

As a witness of the drama, Sarah was going through one of the greatest nightmares of her life. She shook his shoulders a few times to awaken him from trance. Then she kept talking to him to keep his conscious mind alert.

Once again Sarah decided to call me for help.

This was the first time that I had encountered a patient who could self-hypnotize and self-regress easily. It also struck me that Gerald was probably visually psychic to start with. An idea suddenly sparked in my mind ...

While I do not possess clairvoyant qualities myself, I remembered interacting with a visually psychic lady once who gave me the feedback that she could visualize my facial image each time she received thought messages from me.

I knew I was getting into uncharted waters, but decided to conduct an experiment nonetheless. What happened in the next half-hour would be very difficult to understand.

It was 00:03 am. There was no time to lose. I sat back in a quiet corner in my bedroom and took a deep breath. With my eyes closed, I quickly entered into an alpha meditative state myself. With the image of Gerald in my mind I mentally recited a hypnotic induction script! "Take a deep breath slowly, Gerald, and let yourself drift into a calm and peaceful state. From now on you will focus on my voice and get into a state of relaxation."

Suddenly I sensed an overwhelming aura of confidence around me – the conviction that I could hypnotize someone over distance!

Next I checked the result with Sarah through the telephone.

"Is Gerald able to *see* my face or *hear* my thoughts at this very moment? I have just sent him some instructions to relax."

"Yes," Sarah responded. "He saw your face just now. When I asked him to take a few breaths he opened his eyes and told me he could see you." I was thrilled.

"I daren't sleep now as I'm afraid he'll go into trance again," Sarah continued. "He asked me if you are making him feel sleepy. He feels very peaceful now."

Things had worked exactly as I expected. I told Sarah that I was relaxing him over distance. She felt reassured. I continued to deepen his trance state over distance.

It was 00:20 am and I strongly sensed that Gerald had settled down and gone into delta sleep[11]. Over the next few moments Sarah confirmed all my intuitive observations through SMS.

It was a wonderful feeling of achievement!

---

[11] Delta waves are the slowest and highest amplitude brain waves, and delta sleep is our deepest level of sleep.

Chapter Four

Karmic Debt

> "The results of our action are often delayed, even into future lifetimes; we cannot pin down one cause, because any event can be an extremely complicated mixture of many karmas ripening together. So we tend to assume now that things happen to us 'by chance' and when everything goes well, we simply call it 'good luck'."
>
> Sogyal Rinpoche, 2002

Next morning, 24 October, at 7:40 am, Sarah assured me that Gerald was fine and composed. However, she noticed that the act of driving made him go into trance easily. As the front-seat passenger she felt tense and uneasy, always having to distract him regularly: "Please check your left, check your right and the back," she would keep repeating the reminder to him.

Over the phone she called to make an urgent appointment for me to see her husband. Without delay I arranged for them to come to my clinic later that morning.

Gerald and Sarah turned up at my clinic at 11:40 am. Both of them looked weary and tired. Sarah had found the spontaneously triggered trance states too unpredictable to manage. On the other hand Gerald commented half-jokingly that he could now enter his past life at will by simply picking up his drawing pencil!

He emphasized that he repeatedly experienced visions of a rubber plantation but had no idea of the significance of that scene.

After some thought, I decided to use the mental picture as a starting point for identifying an *affect bridge*[12].

"Take a deep breath ... and as you relax I want you to focus on the rubber plantation, the lights on the rubber trees and tell me if there are any feelings associated with it ..."

It turned out that this was all I needed to say to connect Gerald with his past life!

"I see a rubber tapper, tapping a rubber tree. I am looking at him ... it's night time ... I see a concrete pillar and a metal gate ..." (pause)

The rubber plantation belonged to a rich and powerful person in Malaya. The rubber tapper looked like an Indian. The entrance gate to the plantation had two concrete pillars with a wrought iron gate. He saw Chinese characters inscribed on the front of the pillars. From the gate there was a sand path leading to a wooden hut. The hut was well hidden from sight. On its roof were corrugated zinc sheets. The walls were made of wooden planks; Gerald noticed that the wooden walls did not go all the way up to the roof, because there was a need for ventilation. Gerald sensed a foul fecal smell during the regression and inferred that it came from chicken shit.

Inside the hut was a wooden dining table. Gerald could vividly visualize that the four legs of the wooden table were standing inside tin cans half-filled with water. He did not know what the purpose was, but I was fascinated. Countries in the Tropics are notorious for their insect-teeming environment. Having grown up in an ant-infested kampong in my early years, I was reminded of the common village practice of water-filled cans to deter ants from crawling up the wooden legs of the table to access the food placed on top.

---

[12] An *affect bridge* is a tool that the hypnotherapist uses during regression therapy to connect the patient's subconscious mind to a past experience that is of significance to his present problem. More details are given in the Appendix.

Fig. 4: *"I see a wooden hut ... a forest."*

Next he visualized a few Caucasian men inside the hut together with him and Ah Seng. This was the hideout and where his guerilla group secretly met. Gerald even saw an old box-radio transceiver that the group used for wireless communication.

There was a pause and Gerald jumped to another past life scene ...

"It's a hot day ... There is a piece of paper."

"What did you see on the paper?"

"There is a square chop ... and a triangular stamp ..."

I could not understand the significance of this statement then, but the description of the stamps came up in more detail later.

"A lot of people queuing up. I am very, very hungry and very thirsty ... I am queuing on a road. There are thirty people ahead of me ... it's a long queue. There is a traditional Chinese bench placed transversely across the road ... three heads are lying on the bench."

I gave a shudder as I listened to Gerald's description. He had talked about this earlier in one of his flashbacks, but now he was able to fill in the details.

"The blood is still flowing out from the raw neck wound and dripping down to the floor. Their eyes are not closed ... they are staring at me. In one of the heads I see that the tongue is still sticking out."

It sounded as ghastly as a ghoul!

Gerald was caught unexpectedly in a curfew that had just been announced a moment ago. The Japanese soldiers had quickly erected a barricade after killing and beheading a few civilians. Three soldiers armed with rifles were standing behind and next to a table in the center of the road. Just in front of the table were three decapitated heads placed on a wooden bench, exactly like he envisioned the day before in his flashbacks.

A temporary barbed wire fence was erected on one segment of the road. The location looked like the current day Eu Tong Sen

Street[13]. The barbed wire fence was placed in parallel with the row of shop houses. Multiple coils of concertina barbed wire were seen. Gerald was standing at the entry point of the barricade and was at the end of the queue. Beyond the concertina barbed wire fence, he noticed two posters on the street wall. It looked as if the soldiers were on the lookout for someone to arrest.

Singapore fell to the Japanese on 15 February 1942 and thereafter Japanese rule took over until 12 September 1945. As a matter of fact, the Japanese Occupation has brought back nightmares and memories of horror to many Singaporeans till today. During their reign, the Japanese secret military police, the *kempeitai*, committed numerous atrocities against the common people. They created a spy network of informers around the island to help them identify those who were anti-Japanese. The *kempeitai* jail was in Outram, with branches in Stamford Road and Chinatown. Japanese soldiers frequently patrolled the streets and those who failed their inspections were beaten up and taken away to various deserted spots of the island and systematically killed.

"The two heads on the right of the bench belonged to two young short-haired, Chinese men," Gerald continued. "The one on the left has a high forehead ... an extremely high forehead ... with long hair. He is about sixty years old."

Gerald remembered the scene of the protruding tongue very vividly. He saw the tongue sticking out slightly from the right corner of the mouth and the tongue color still looked fresh. The man's eyes were half-open. He was dark and looked elderly. A chill was going through Gerald's body. As the regression progressed, he

---

[13] Eu Tong Sen Street is a one-way street located in the central part of Singapore linking the areas of Outram, Singapore River and Bukit Merah. It is named after a tycoon who was a mine, rubber estate and property owner.

gradually identified three headless human bodies lying motionless on the ground.

"Their bodies are at the side of the road and they have been shot. The two younger bodies are each dressed in singlet and shorts," he said.

"The third body belongs to the older man and is dressed in long pants and long-sleeved shirt ... a traditional Chinese shirt." Apparently this body belonged to the man with the high forehead and long hair.

"What else did you see?"

"I see a triangular stamp. The chop is on the three bodies ... There are two types of stamps, a triangular and a square. There are words on the stamp, but I don't understand them ..."

The Japanese officers were singling out "suspicious" characters at their whims and fancy. Those who survived the inspection walked away with a square ink stamp on their arms. The unfortunate ones who failed the inspection would be stamped with triangular marks instead and were taken away.

Apparently this was part of a massacre called Sook Ching Operation, which essentially was a systematic extermination of perceived hostile elements among the Singapore Chinese. The Malayan Peninsula and the southern island of Singapore were British colonies then. The Japanese military had viewed all China-born Chinese who migrated to Malaya-Singapore after the second Sino-Japanese War as undesirable elements. In addition, all men with tattoos were assumed to be Chinese Triad members and would be arrested.

"Oh, they are checking more on the men," Gerald said.

"Who are they?"

"These are people who each wear a white band over their right arms. They are Chinese ..."

What Gerald described were local Singaporean Chinese civilians working for the Japanese soldiers. Under continuing pressure from the Japanese military, some local Singaporean Chinese would volunteer to provide information on who were supposedly anti-Japanese. The reward for the volunteer job would vary from promises of special treatment to open threats of execution for themselves or their family members.

Fig. 5: "He's the one who tortured me." (Gerald's drawing)

"But there is one Japanese officer among them. He is carrying a samurai sword and has a small moustache on his upper lip ..."

"There is another Japanese officer wearing round-framed spectacles ... quite skinny ... he's bald. Looks like he's a senior officer. They are greeting him."

"What happened next?"

"The queue now splits into two, with the males on one side and the females on the other side. I sense danger. I walk out of the queue ... I'm afraid."

"What are you afraid of?"

"They are catching all the males. They are checking on them ... I am not at the queue now. I am looking at them from the side of the shop house."

"What else did you see?"

"They make all the males take off their clothes. That guy has a tattoo. They take a sword and chop off his head, without saying anything."

Gerald started to writhe in pain.

"They open fire. Everyone is running. They give us an order: *Don't run! Everybody squat down!*"

Gerald had started crying at this stage.

"They are rounding up all those men with tattoos."

"How many men are there with tattoos?"

"Five ... Any tattoo ... no matter where, be it on the legs, hand, or back ... all those with tattoos are arrested."

"What did they do to the five people they arrested?"

"One of them tries to escape. The soldier uses the rifle to hit him and the bayonet to stab him. The other four don't dare to move. They pierce him, pierce him and pierce him ... The Japanese general chops off his head. Now there are five heads on the street."

The voice now changed to one of fear.

"I don't know what they are queuing for. Going to get killed? I am scared. I walk away and start to run. They are shouting at me ... They are opening fire at me.

"I run ... Just run, don't care ... run." Gerald was gasping in fear. His breathing turned heavy and then he began to pant.

"Where are you running to?"

"Just run, don't care, just run ..."

From what I understood from Gerald's subsequent research, Mei Fung's residence was at Duxton Road[14] and located within a two-kilometer radius from the *kempeitai*. From the site of the public beheading in Eu Tong Sen Street, he ran across Smith Street and found his way to Mei Fung's residence at Duxton Road.

"They are chasing me. I run upstairs ... no idea which building I am in ... I see a walkway with wooden floor. There are many rooms on both sides. I see an old lady."

"Do you know her?"

"Yes. She is Mei Fung's mother. She asks me why the Japanese soldiers are coming at us. I say to her that they are killing people. She tells me to quickly bring Mei Fung home. She's outside ... washing clothes. I go downstairs to look for her. I see Ah Seng ... he is cooking noodles in his stall, next to mine. He puts fifty cents on my counter ... he just sold two bottles of soft drinks for me while I was away."

"What happened next?"

"I am going to the washing point to find Mei Fung ..."

In the old Chinatown days, it was a practice to have water dispensing points in public. At these points were pumps that needed to be activated before the taps could supply water for laundry purposes. The women would gather together on such spots to wash clothes in the open.

"She's not there." Gerald sounded anxious and disappointed.

"Where is she?"

"I am going to another spot to look for her. Maybe this tap failed to dispense water and she has gone to another washing point ..." (pause)

---

[14] Duxton Road in old Singapore is an area where rickshaw pullers park their vehicles at the end of the day. Opium and gambling dens as well as cheap brothels used to flourish in the area. In modern times, the place has been conserved by the Urban Redevelopment Authority. Many refurbished two- and three-storey houses are seen in the area today.

Fig. 6: "The street where I used to sell drinks in my past life."

"Are you there now?"

"I am still walking there. It's quite a distance."

"Go to the point when you arrived at your destination."

"Everybody is running away. The Japanese soldiers are coming ... They are catching someone. Everyone is running away ... I can't find Mei Fung. I can't find her." He sighed. "Where can she be? ... Where did she go?" Gerald sounded as panicky as a deer that is being predated upon.

"What happened next?"

"I couldn't find her ... I come back to my store ... I see a lady." (sigh)

"Who is she?"

"She's Mei Fung. She is arrested by the Japanese soldiers. Two of the soldiers take her away."

"What happened next?"

"Mei Fung's mother falls down the stairs. Her scalp is bleeding ... wow ... a lot of blood! Mei Fung is out of sight already."

At this point, still in deep trance, Gerald suddenly spoke in Hokkien[15], his native dialect.

"Ah Seng, will you manage Auntie first ... Auntie, do you want to go to the *sinseh* first? ... Why not? ... There is a lot of bleeding ... are you feeling giddy now? Better get help from the *sinseh* now.

"Too much bleeding now. I apply pressure on the wound."

Next Gerald carried the old lady on his back to seek medical help.

"She is very heavy ... Don't worry about Mei Fung, I will bring her back. Get your medical treatment first. I promise I will bring her back."

Mei Fung's mother took out a piece of red paper with the daughter's birth data written on it (traditionally known as *BaZi*).

"What is the *BaZi*[16] for? Let me bring you for medical attention first. Stop worrying ... I promise I will save her ... Nothing will happen to her."

It was an impossible promise that Gerald made to Mei Fung's mother at the heat of the moment, and one which he couldn't fulfill in the end.

"Ah Seng, please close your hawker store and help to bring her to the *sinseh*. I don't know what the paper is for ... I couldn't read Chinese."

"What happened next?"

---

[15] There was a large influx of Chinese migrants from Southern China in the 19th and early 20th centuries. Many of these migrants came from the province of Fujian and brought the Hokkien dialect to Singapore. Many private Chinese schools used Hokkien as the medium of instruction until it was replaced by Mandarin in the early 20th century.

[16] *BaZi* literally means Eight Characters. It refers to the astrological identity of the individual based on the birth data.

"She is bleeding badly. She shows me a piece of paper ... one side of the paper is red colored. On the other side is written: *Seventh Month & Twenty-First day of the Lunar Calendar*. It looks like Mei Fung's birthday. There are a few other words but I can't read and don't understand."

"What happened next?"

"She doesn't want medical attention. She's crying. She is very weak. I think she is dying. She's lost too much blood. She tells me to rescue Mei Fung and take good care of her." (pause)

There appeared a sudden flash of insight on Gerald's part. "I now know why the Japanese came to get her. They wanted to catch me ... because I ran upstairs and they couldn't find and catch me, they caught Mei Fung instead." Gerald suddenly felt as guilty as a puppy sitting beside a pile of poo.

At this point I recalled Gerald telling me earlier of his dreams about himself running up and down a staircase. It seemed that his past life guilt had been carried over to the present life.

During the next few moments, Gerald was crying very emotionally. However, I believed this new insight was the turning point in his healing.

"I get her into all this. I must save her. I get her daughter into trouble. If I had not run upstairs it would not be her but me who is arrested (sigh) ... I have got her into trouble."

Suddenly there was another turning point in the story.

"Auntie is dead ... Auntie is dead." Gerald went into full-blown catharsis[17].

In my training it is a common practice to actively assist a patient in catharsis to release his emotions. Suppressing emotions during regression therapy is considered akin to building bombs. It

---

[17] Catharsis is an emotional release associated with talking about the underlying causes of a problem. The term is used in psychotherapy to describe the act of experiencing the deep emotions associated with the events of an individual's past.

is often said that when a patient buries his emotions, he is perceived to have buried them alive!

"Mei Fung got caught. I must save her. Bloody Japanese soldiers (sniffing) … I must kill them all. They have killed so many innocent people."

"What happened next?"

"Ah Seng stops me … I want to kill them … I want to take revenge … Please don't stop me … I want to kill them … why are you stopping me? Don't you see what they did? I know I'm stupid … but do you know where are they taking Mei Fung to? What if they abuse her?"

I noted the agonizing state that Gerald was in. He appeared like a scorpion stung by his own rage. His clenched fist was clutching the blanket tightly, while fine hand tremors were increasingly visible. The tendons on the dorsum of his right hand tensed up in a fan-like pattern while the superficial veins over the hand were engorged with blood, as if ready to burst and spurt. Anger filled the air. I heard the soft gritting sound of his teeth.

I waited a couple of minutes and asked: "What is happening now?"

"Everything is white … I see a hospital bed. Mei Fung is on it, crying. She's smiling at me. I am hugging her now."

Gerald's arms rose and opened up. I passed him a pillow and he hugged it passionately. It was imperative at this point to help him bring himself to a satisfactory resolution to release his guilt.

"Is there anything you want to say to her that you did not have a chance to say earlier?"

"Sorry, I caused you to get caught by the Japanese," Gerald spoke in Mandarin this time. "Had I not run upstairs you would not have been caught. Sorry, Mei Fung. I did not expect they would take you away instead of me. I got you and your mum in trouble … forgive me … sorry … sorry …"

"How did she respond?"

"She is crying ..." Gerald switched back to speaking English. "And now smiling ... She doesn't blame me. She's glad that we see each other again," he said with a sigh.

"Give her a good hug, and when you are ready, say goodbye to her. And if you need to cry, please let it out."

Gerald went into catharsis once more and kept crying for several minutes.

"Take care of yourself." He finally bid farewell to Mei Fung.

I decided to end the session then, but getting Gerald out of trance was no easy matter. He experienced a lot of reluctance in opening his eyelids. He had just experienced one of life's hardest lessons: Much as we want to, we can't always protect those we love or ourselves from getting hurt in real life.

Sometimes it is inevitable that we lose loved ones to death no matter where we are or what we do. Things can go wrong and our lives change. It is a universal reality that we are surrounded by loss and suffering of change. The aim of therapy is to remove guilt and free the patient from the anger that results from past injustice. It was an opportunity for Gerald to work through a past life trauma, discover common life themes and synthesize these themes into a meaningful whole. He was aware that he would never completely wipe out the memory of his past life grief and losses, and perhaps he didn't really want to. He had obtained forgiveness from Mei Fung. He seemed keen to conserve meaningful memories and feelings and to find courage and fortitude to coexist peacefully with his losses.

This past life lesson has illustrated the *doctrine of change*. It is the belief that there is a perpetual flux of all things. There is no permanence attached to any of them, not even individual existence. This implies a human life that is on-flowing. Out of this principle is derived the belief that man's eternal career depends on his karma or action. Gerald's deed in his past life had left traces on his present life character. He had left behind a *karmic debt* which stemmed from a negative event involving interpersonal relationships in his past life. This needed to be addressed in the present life to generate peace and wellbeing.

Ever since Gerald's second session, his psychic ability had become increasingly obvious. Now and again Sarah would mention examples of his psychic sensibilities. There was once I was at home reflecting over Gerald's past life story and he immediately picked up my thoughts telepathically. Next he would call me to confirm: "Doc, are you sending me thought messages now? It was a ringing tone that I heard ... and I see a visual image of you. I am actually at work now and then I received a signal, so immediately I decided to ask if you are looking for me."

In the weeks that followed, Gerald's psychic ability became increasingly uncanny ...

Chapter Five

Unfinished Business

"For a long time it had seemed to me that life was about to begin – real life. But there was always some obstacle in the way, something to be gotten through first, some unfinished business, time still to be served, a debt to be paid. Then life would begin. At last it dawned on me that these obstacles were my life.

Alfred D. Souza

A month later Gerald made up his mind to change jobs. His dislike of the backstabbing corporate environment and his disgust of being betrayed by his colleagues at work had been a push factor. He was also very keen to move on in life.

At noon on 28 November, he was sitting on his sofa typing his resume on his laptop computer. Suddenly he felt a fainting sensation. There were no obvious triggers, no ringing sounds in the ear, nausea, palpitations nor any other prodromal symptoms that he could recall. At this point he had a distinct feeling of "falling down a flight of stairs". He woke up an hour later from his unconscious state and found his laptop lying on the floor.

The next day Gerald had another similar blackout while looking at a discarded mirror in his mother-in-law's house. This worried Sarah. Along with the syncope, he again experienced the nagging feeling of grappling with some *unfinished business*. Sarah was increasingly concerned and keen that he should seek answers promptly to his unresolved issues. However, he procrastinated.

Finally, on 2 February 2012 Gerald turned up at my clinic with a wry smile. He asked for a third therapy session.

This time, I used his syncopal attacks as the starting point for identifying an affect bridge. With his eyes closed and his mind focused on his most recent blackout, I prompted him to allow an associated emotion to surface. After a while, a feeling of fear emerged. He then rapidly slipped into trance with minimal facilitation on my part.

"Dunking ... underwater ... fear ..." Gerald began. "I feel like dying ... I can't breathe." Gerald's body muscles began to tense up.

"I regret taking this path," he murmured.

"What path are you referring to?" I asked.

"The anti-Japanese path," he replied. (pause) "Betrayal ... someone in the group betrayed me. We went into hiding in Muar.[18] Not many people know. A group went searching for our hideout. Only two of us were hiding."

The past life link that explained his strong dislike for corporate backstabbing and the desire to change jobs became increasingly obvious.

"We are all running ... all forest ... all trees ... rubber plantations in Johor. The soldiers are chasing us." He took a deep breath.

"A river ... quite deep. We try to swim across. Ouch ... my legs cramp." He took another heavy breath as his facial muscles tensed up.

"My buddy tries to pull me out of the water. I tell him to go ... but he comes back to me." Anxiety grew on his face.

"Oh ... the soldiers open fire and shoot him! He struggles ... but he cannot make it ... he's going to die." Pain filled his voice in addition to the disappointment on his face.

---

[18] Muar is a district in the state of Johor, Malaysia.

Fig. 7: The hideout in Muar

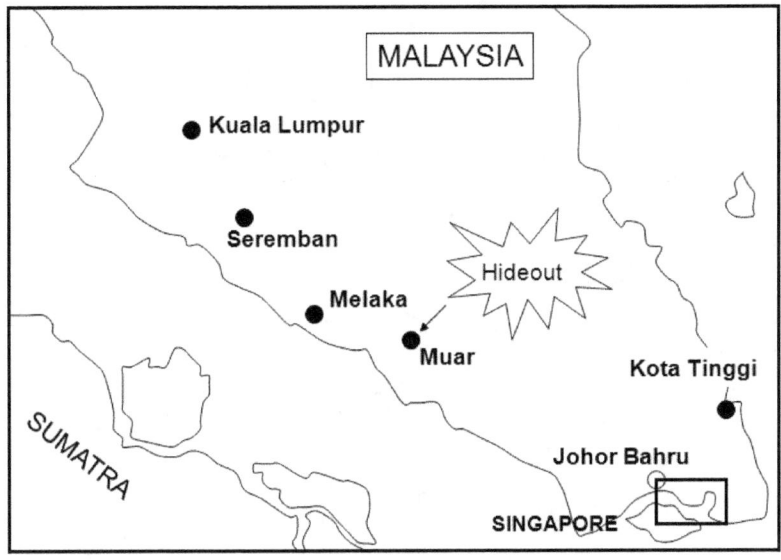

"They do not shoot at me because they want to see me drown. I am trying to float ... washed away by the current ... he drifts away from me. He's gone ... he's dead. The soldiers come down on me. I am captured by them. If not for me, he wouldn't have died. I feel very sorry. I want to know the one who betrayed me and I want to kill him!"

The voice was saturated with guilt and hatred.

"The cell ... high ceiling ... high wall, suspended lights ... walls in blue and white. The Japanese officer is with me ... watching me being tortured. He's skinny and bald. He wears spectacles, he is small and with a moustache."

Through his subsequent research Gerald found out that this Japanese officer whom he saw and who tortured him was Colonel Masanobu Tsuji, the primary mastermind of the Sook Ching Operation. Tsuji was well known not only for his role in the massacre of Chinese civilians in Singapore but for many other war crimes during the Pacific War. However, he managed to escape trial after the war.

Fig. 8: *Pulau Serangoon (Coney Island) and the execution spot*

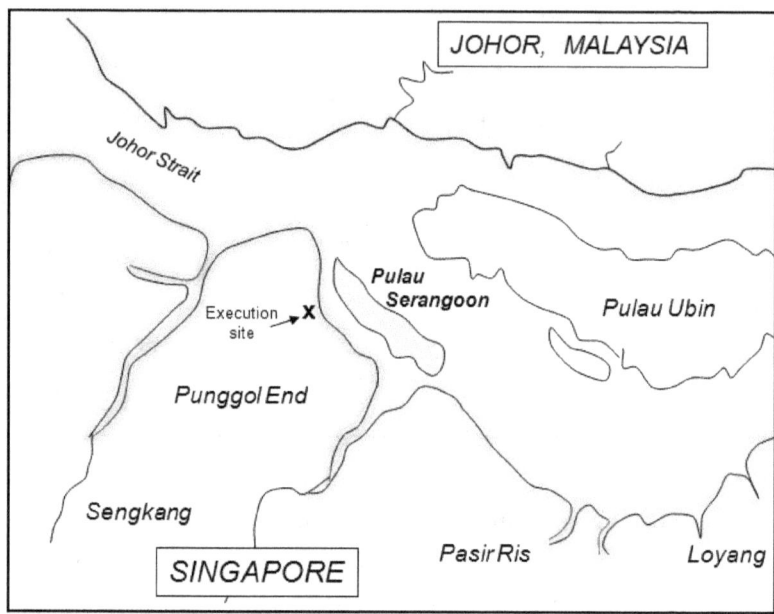

"He [Col. Tsuji] is trying to find out who funds the guerilla force. I say nothing. They use a knife to slash me each time I remain silent. They are asking about the place where we kept our weapons. I don't know so much. My task is only spying and assassination.

"I have no idea how they know my whereabouts. In the course of my spying, I collect information about who helped the Japanese to establish military secrets. They are usually Chinese merchants. These merchants help to sell the secrets to the Imperial Army. Nothing much we can do about it. The Japanese are aggressive. They show me an execution of a fellow Chinese traitor in the form of public beheading. They take people out to the street and make them kneel down. Using the sharp Japanese sword they behead them as a warning to others who are going against them. Sooner or later, it will be my turn. I know there isn't a lot of time.

"Why can't I just be a normal person? I am betrayed and can never beat the Japanese. I feel foolish. At this point I feel I am a coward ... afraid to die. It's the fear, just the fear ... I am waiting for them to kill me. Even if I tell them the truth they will still kill me. To tell or not to tell, I'll still die.

"Don't be foolish to give in to them. They will still kill you ..." Gerald uttered to himself in deep trance.

"So I do not give in to them. They continue to torture me. They continue to use the knife to slash my body. Then they sprinkle salt on my wound! The torture tactic that I fear most is the dunking. They won't kill me ... just want my head under water for a couple of seconds.

"Drowning ... water got into my nose, mouth. I couldn't breathe. I don't like the sound of underwater.

"I am on a truck to somewhere, blindfolded. I can smell the sea. They have brought us to the beach ... hot sand, it is a hot day.

"Today is the day. All the torture will stop. I feel fearful because I am going to die and I also feel relieved because everything is going to be over. Not sure how many of us are there - we are all kneeling on the sand. Some are Indians and I hear Malays too. They are saying prayers now. They all know we're going to die. Everyone is fearful. Somehow we feel it. We know we are going to die. Sad ... regret ...!

"I am asking myself why I do all these things. I tell myself I am doing the right thing - to stop evil and stand up for every Chinese man who has been killed and tortured. Poor Mei Fung, I am doing this for her. I caused her death. If not for me she would not have died. If I am not from the guerilla force both of us wouldn't die. I feel sad because I'm betrayed. I am not able to forgive the person who betrayed me."

Fig. 9: "This is the spot where I was executed!"

"Next is the execution ... 'Bang' ... and that's it. The shot travels through my body. I feel a sense of shock and a little bit of pain from the bullet shot. I feel numb all over the body, cold, shocked. Everything is fast ...

"I see myself now. Collapsed on the sand, bleeding from the left chest. Hair quite long, tanned and skinny."

As he was leaving his body and rising upwards, he saw a scene of the same island which he had visualized in his previous flashbacks.

"There is an island, opposite the beach. This place looks very familiar. The island is very close to the beach. A lot of trees at the shoreline. Short, pointing trees ... look like casuarinas trees. Everything is white. I can't see anything. I feel very relieved. The island looks familiar in current life. Looks like Pulau Serangoon (renamed Coney Island) in the current life. It's sited off Punggol End."

Fig. 10: "House with white roof, sampan ... resembles exactly the image I saw in my regression!"

"A few small boats ... sampan. There's a small Malay village and small house. I've been there before. I was on a trip to spy on the Japanese. A young man was giving fish to the Japanese. He looked like my grandfather. I was hiding behind some lalang to see how the Japanese bring in resources from Malaya. The intention was to hijack their goods for our own usage, but we were not successful. This man had a *kelong*. We believed he was very familiar with Japanese routine because of the frequency of the shipment coming to Singapore. He was not part of our guerilla group. His relationship with the Japanese was very good. He didn't want trouble and did not cooperate with us. (sigh) He gave his fish to the Japanese so that they would be nice to him.

Fig. 11: The execution spot in present-day Punggol Point

"We had the intention to poison the Japanese via the sea food using puffer-fish poison. We asked him for puffer fish. He refused. He did not want to cause trouble. He just wanted to lead a normal life. We eventually gave up asking him.

"We tried to hijack their ship but we were always outnumbered by them. We succeeded in collecting information but I had never killed a single Japanese soldier with my own hands. I felt useless ... I should have killed at least one or two of them. We just do spying and target those who betray the British Army."

Gerald drifted away to another familiar scene at this point.

"I am in front of a hospital bed. Mei Fung is waiting for me. Tears roll out on her cheek. We hug each other. We meet once again. She has forgiven me. She has never been angry or ever blamed me. (sigh) I feel good."

"What are the patterns you have noticed in this past life that are related to your current life?" I asked.

"It is the fear of water ..." he said. "Also, I don't like to run."

Before I could ask further, Gerald spontaneously connected with another past life link.

"Everything is white ... there's a door, a gate ... I walk through it and fall down a flight of steps. It's like the fainting spells I had recently ... it's the same kind of feeling."

It was fascinating. I remembered exactly how he described to me this same feeling of falling down the stairs when he last fainted while typing his resume.

"In front of me suddenly everything is very dark. I am in an enclosed space. It is very dark, and I feel lost. I try to find a way out. I climb the stairs and I keep climbing and climbing. Just can't complete the climbing. I feel very lost ... At last it gets brighter and brighter and I see the gate again. No idea where the gate leads to."

"Describe the gate to me," I said.

"The gate is made of metal ... tall, round, with a long arch. The top of the gate is curved. It's a metallic gray color. Looks like an ancient gate."

"Is it the same gate that you saw when you had your near death experience in your early childhood?" I eagerly asked.

"No, it's not the same gate."

"Anyone else with you?"

"At the other side of the gate is a lady with a flower basket. She is a Caucasian lady, smiling at me. She waves to me, telling me to go away ... You don't belong here, she says."

"She looks like a chambermaid wearing a white apron, with something tied to her head. She scatters the flower petals across the gate. She's laying the path with flower petals to welcome people into the other dimension but she says the place is not for me. She gestures me to go away."

"I leave. Everything is white. I see Mei Fung again. We are walking around. I tell her at last we have each other's company and she agrees. Mei Fung tells me she tried entering the gate also but was rejected ... Just like me."

I was curious. "Ask your spirit guide why this happened."

"We have not got through our fate yet. Mei Fung has committed suicide. It's a sin. She has to live her life all over again through reincarnation. For me, I've to find the answer to our unfinished business. I have to grapple with the guilt I have with Mei Fung and the anger I have to the one who betrayed me ...

"No matter who you are, it's past. The more I find out, the worse I become. I'm willing to forgive. Release me of all this pain (sigh) ... and finish with all this unfinished business."

I ended the session at this point after guiding Gerald through some healing visual imagery.

Sarah messaged me the same evening to say that Gerald felt so exhausted after the therapy that he couldn't recall much of what went on during the session. He did remember, however, that he "forgave that someone". I took that to mean he had forgiven the person who betrayed him in his past life.

A month later, Gerald tried spraying the water on his face during his shower. Nothing happened to him. He took it calmly!

"Hi, Doc. I did try to use water to splash onto my face," he wrote to me. "It was amazing because when water got into my nostrils, there was no panicky fear which I used to have!"

He felt like he had undergone a conversion in his life. The therapy sessions had provided him opportunities for self-cleansing. Next comes self-forgiveness, and finally a self-renewal is in sight.

"Thank you very much for the regression therapy and for healing my illness. This experience is very fruitful in my search for my purpose in my past and current life. I am sure I can start to learn swimming soon."

Two months later, Gerald made a visit to Punggol End. He looked at Pulau Serangoon (Coney Island) with mixed feelings. There was a sense of déjà vu. Flashbacks of his past life guerilla activities occurred as he looked at the island. A couple of casuarinas trees and a few sampans spontaneously appeared in his vision, and were superimposed on his image of the island. He quietly stood there and identified the spot where he was executed. The site had been redeveloped for tourists but he felt as if he had been there before, with a strong sense of emotional association.

The following day he went for an exploratory expedition in the present-day Chinatown. He drove past Duxton Road and suddenly had a sense of familiarity, of having been there before. He got down from the car and saw in front of him the row of shop houses that corresponded to where he used to sell drinks in his past life. The structural appearance of the houses was identical to what he had visualized during the regression. The unit where Mei Fung stayed had been refurbished into a shop with a signboard showing "Pub Seventeen". The sense of familiarity was so strong that he took a snapshot of the place and emailed to me.

With his past life behind him, Gerald had since moved on. He was employed in a new job with a medical appliance company, something that he was very excited about. He had always wanted to be part of the helping community and he now felt that this job was heading him in the direction he had been working towards.

Section B

A Call for Action

Chapter Six

Procrastination

"Often a personality experiences effects that were created by other of its soul's personalities and, conversely, creates energy imbalances that are not able to right themselves within its own lifetime. Therefore, without knowledge of its soul, reincarnation, and karma, it is not always possible for a personality to understand the significance or the meaning of the events of its life, or to understand the effects of its responses to them."

Gary Zukav, 1989

An unsolicited email came to me one day from Milton. He had heard of my hypnotherapy practice through his wife who is a nurse. For several years, he had been grappling with the problems of procrastination and anger. He had been trying particularly hard for the past year to contain his anger and finally decided that he needed a therapist's help.

He appeared in my clinic on the afternoon of 15 November 2011. Handsome-looking and about six feet in height, he was in his mid-forties. He had thick black hair with a parting just slightly to the left of the midline. He lost no time in getting to the root of his clinical problem. Expressive and keen to share, he talked about his issues in depth.

Procrastination had haunted him for the past seventeen years. The problem worsened each time he was on a big project, be it within his job or his business venture. He had a peculiar tendency to slow down to a halt each time his campaign was near success and fruition. Whenever he had to face a difficult situation, he would choose to browse the Internet rather than to face and tackle the problem at hand. Although at work he was reporting to a manager who would whip him forward for the final lap, it would still take a lot of whipping or a huge incentive before he could break the inertia.

Milton had three sons, aged ten, nine and seven years of age. He tended to have outbursts of anger with them, even for the most minor issues and in the absence of a clear reason. He hated this because it built walls between him and his children. Also he couldn't figure out why he possessed an unexplainable fear of losing them.

Initially I wasn't quite clear if Milton was just one of those individuals who liked to take life easy and needed a long time to get things done or if he had a real problem. However, he recalled that even during his student years, he was good in coming up with ideas but tended to flounder when it came to executing the project.

Currently the procrastination seemed to have taken a toll on his career, work and life. At a personal level, he was moving away further and further from his dreams of achieving career independence because of this undesirable habit. Yet, from an observer's viewpoint, he looked more like a naturally relaxed person. For a moment I wondered if he was just simply putting things off rather than truly procrastinating.

Milton eventually revealed that he had previously sought therapy from various sources but experienced no improvement. In the past years, he had also attended several motivational workshops and seminars but the impact of what he learned in those events was short-lasting.

It began to affect him badly in 1994. A business venture failed that year and he didn't feel like facing the truth. The situation was aggravated because of his second problem of anger management.

His anger spells started during school days. He used to take a shuttle service from his housing estate to get to his secondary school every morning. On most rides, he felt that the bus was extremely slow and was frequently furious with the driver. On an average, he flared up two or three times a week as a passenger. At first he thought the temper situation was restricted to himself and the bus driver. As he grew up he was increasingly aware that he had difficulty controlling his anger. This was pointed out by his wife one day.

During the year when his business was not doing well, his anger outbursts at his mum could be nerve-racking, despite the fact that he loved her a lot. Three sessions of hypnotherapy with a private therapist in 2004 did not improve the situation.

It was 2:45 pm. After hearing Milton's story, I felt that I should be able to help him. He was relaxed on a reclining couch, and I guided him quickly into a hypnotic state through deep breathing. Using a progressive relaxation script with guided imagery, I got him to drift into a dream-like state and he was feeling very peaceful. After half an hour of hypnotic relaxation I decided to deepen him with the help of the fractionation[19] effect.

"As you drift off into a dreamy state, Milton, I want you to imagine yourself being in a safe place that you have chosen for yourself."

I had chosen to establish a safe place for Milton before starting regression therapy. This preliminary step is frequently critical for success, so I was taught. A place that is peaceful and safe

---

[19] Fractionation is carried out by inducing the patient into a light level of hypnosis, letting him come out of it for a moment and then relaxing him back into a hypnotic state once more. The second time the patient enters hypnosis, he would enter it at a deeper level.

for the patient to go to at any time during the session and that nobody else could get into, will provide the security needed by the patient should the therapy become tough going later.

"It is a place where you feel safe and comfortable," I continued. "It is free from anxiety, and is a place that you really like to be in because it is so peaceful and quiet ..." After a short while, his ideomotor finger response affirmed that he was in his chosen place. He then told me he was in his bedroom.

"Stay there ... and I want you to go back to the last time when you felt irritated with your problem of procrastination, the way you were waiting for things to be done and yet not doing it ... and now tell me the emotion associated with the situation."

"Frustration."

"Focus on the feeling of frustration and amplify it. I will help you by counting from one to ten and with each count you will double your level of frustration. One, two, three, four ... ten and you find yourself at maximum intensity of that emotion. And now as I count backwards from ten to one you will drift back in time to an event when you experienced the same emotion. Ten, nine, eight, seven, ... one. Allow the images to form in your mind, and, at your own time and pace, tell me what you see and what you are doing now."

"I am in the previous job," he said. "There were many calls that I refused to make, resulting in the loss of a deal. This was in 2003. I was in a taxi. I was boarding a taxi in front of my old house. I got a message on my Blackberry to tell me that I had lost the deal."

"What were your thoughts then?"

"I asked myself why it happened again." He gave a little sigh.

"What were the emotions associated with this thought?"

"Disappointment ... and tension," he said without hesitation.

"That time I was running a printing business. The same thing happened in 1992. There was a deal that I did not follow up ... I am in the old factory set up. I am by the old desk ... in a room, sitting on a chair ... mulling over the new machines I just bought. Those are the big printing machines. The deal comes. I do not follow up on it. Things start to unravel ... taking up more projects ... under capacity. Certain parts of the business are doing well but the printing business is not doing as well as expected. "

"How do you feel at this stage?"

"Anxiety ... because I know I am heading for doom. I was naïve and bold. (pause) I can feel a bit of regret and a bit of sadness. Things could have turned the other way round if I had taken enough action. I had not followed advice from my seniors and veterans in the industry. My uncle said I was a bit too headstrong. I knew better. I wasn't too pleased."

"What happened next?"

"I continued to make certain silly mistakes in the business. I ran short of funds. I couldn't keep up with the cash flows. I started to employ illegal workers then, to reduce the cost. It helped for a little while until I was busted. There was a peak of production and I was running a 24-hour shift. It lasted about four to six months. (sigh) There was a raid by the police. They stopped my operations. I shut the factory. Debt issues mounted ... I sold off everything. I did not do anything for months."

"And what emotions were you having then?"

"Fear ... because of legal pursuit." The fact that the delay had resulted in both internal distress as well as serious legal issues left no doubts in my mind that the procrastination had reached pathological levels.

'What thoughts go with the fear?'

"What will happen next? Can I handle it? Each time I asked these questions there was more fear than frustration ... fear of not doing what is in front of me."

"What happened next?"

"The state of fear lasted one and a half to two years. I did nothing in the meanwhile. I was out with friends pretending to be happy and putting on a front. Each time I put on a front, I told myself that this is happening for a reason.

"What is the reason behind this?"

"I was unhappy. I was pretty ugly ... ugly in my state of mind and my approach for money. (sigh) I was bribing to get business done. I wasn't happy. I told myself things will be sorted out."

"Did things get sorted out in the end?"

"Somehow ... many years later. The police busting my factory was the trigger for everything else. I was completely paralyzed by fear ... Oh shit! ... when I first received the call."

"How did you continue to handle this fear?"

"It took me half an hour to get out of the bed at that time."

It sounded bad. "What happened next?" I asked.

"After I got out of bed, I took my time and dressed up to go back to the factory to see what happened. Six guys were being caught. They were all my workers. I have no idea what happened to them. I was asked to go back to the Ministry of Manpower. (sigh) I was asked to sit there for a long time until the investigator came to the room."

"Describe the room to me."

"There was a desk. The room had maroon walls. There was nobody else. On the adjacent side of the desk was another chair. There were police files on the table. I was caught red-handed. I waited for a long time. (sigh) Eventually a female investigator came. She asked me what happened. I told her it's my mistake. She said she had to wait for a while, for the letters from the Ministry of Manpower to come. I was asked to leave.

"I engaged a litigation lawyer. He managed to bargain off for a fine instead of a jail term. One out of five of the workers was an illegal immigrant. The rest were students. It was pretty good relief.

(sigh) I had to look for money to pay for the fine too. I went to court. The lawyers were talking. I was fined thirty thousand dollars."

"How did you feel when you heard about the fine?"

"Relieved ... and also burdened, because of the money. I was completely negative then. (sigh) I raised the money and paid off the fine. The bigger looming question was how to pay off the rest of my debts. I had no answer to the question myself. I delayed with the banks ... restructured the loans and restructured the debts. I am still paying today. When I thought about it, it was a stupid decision resulting in a very heavy burden."

"What happened next?"

"I got a job two years down the road. In the first job, half the time I was selling an IT system - a very rudimentary accounting system. The job wasn't too bad. The problem was with the boss. It was freelance sales ... only paid on commission and no basic pay ... couldn't really make a living. Then I closed a bigger sale for the entire company and the boss didn't pay me!

"Then I moved into insurance. During the job I realized my sales technique wasn't too good. I thought selling insurance might be the way to learn some hard-core sales technique. I stayed around for a while and made a few sales. I was in insurance for nearly one year before the 1997 Asian Financial Crisis hit. Nobody bought anything. Everybody was watching their purse. Tons of people were retrenched. All the phone calls and hard knocks turned out to be zero sales for a long time. To survive I had to move on."

"How did you move on?"

"I got another job with a basic salary. It was an HR recruitment job, helping the company set up IT recruitment, recruiting specialized IT staff. The job wasn't too bad but the politics was way too heavy. I was in the job for one to one and a half years."

"What made you leave?"

"They told me to leave. The reason they gave was that I wasn't too suitable for it ... but because the instructions did not come from the big boss, I adamantly stayed. Then I found something new one and a half months later. I was on my path to where I am today. I was back to a small IT firm selling IT systems. Again I managed to sell the biggest system they ever sold at the time.

"One year later I found another job. I stayed for five to six years. The company went through multiple downsizing and cost-cutting. I managed to stay because of my performance, I suppose, until it was finally acquired by another company. I realized I couldn't work with this new merger and acquisition and I had to move back to my previous company. Then I did alright in the sales but realized I was not in an environment that I wanted. It was a very technical company whereas my skills are in software application and sales.

"In three and half years I joined another company because I felt this was a better choice. The new job was not too bad. I performed consistently over changing targets. I began doing the biggest sales the division had ever done. I felt good. It was the first time I saw I was able to clear my debts. I felt quite excited that there was a path to clear my debts. But I also realized that this was very dependent on others having the ability to perform.

"I was getting tired. It was not sustainable. Age was catching up. I couldn't run as fast as before. I didn't feel too bad about that. I was more discerning, less cynical with my words and less critical."

"What happened next?"

"So I delved into other business opportunities but did not fall out too well again. I also dabbled into Internet businesses but did not follow through. I was waiting, sitting on my butt, not doing anything beyond what had been done. On the other side, work continued to excel. On a personal basis and personal finance side I was not doing that great ... mediocre. That's why I am here now. I want to make a change."

I was alerted. The last sentence brought me right back to the original purpose of our session, that what he really needed was healing.

"Thank you for describing all these experiences. The next thing I want you to do is go a bit deeper in your trance." I followed up with a healing script.

"As you go deep, you will find the inner calm within yourself. You will be able to manage your anger and focus better. And as I speak to you, you will be more and more receptive subconsciously to the suggestions that I give you. They will begin to build a fortress block by block, stone by stone, and you will build your life now to the great success and the person you want to be."

While there are many ways of formulating hypnotic suggestions, I had begun the script by the use of enriching metaphors.

"From now onwards you will be a person on time and always prepared for your job. You will find that, beginning now, you are becoming more success oriented. There will be no one who can keep you away from the success that you want and you will feel a sense of enthusiasm and confidence in living with new attitudes every day.

"You know in yourself you are overcoming your procrastination because you want to. You are taking a great deal of pride in the fact that you are mature. And you are taking control of your life and beginning to do the things you put off in the past. Your fear, nervousness and all your past struggles are things you leave behind. You leave your old habits behind and make yourself more organized so much so that it becomes more natural for yourself. Now you feel a new healthier sense of accomplishment as you cross off your list of chores and responsibilities one by one."

As a rule, positive suggestions are more readily accepted by the subconscious mind than negative ones. As I proceeded, I subtly repeated the suggestions in different forms to maximize the effect.

"Perhaps you procrastinated when you faced something that you didn't want to do. Until now you put those jobs off. Now you do them. You feel a sense of urgency to complete and succeed in the things that need to be done. You realize that to become the radiant person you want to be you have to take care of some of the unpleasant things and you have to tackle them like the sparkling adult you really are.

"You refuse to let jobs pile up on you anymore. You feel a wonderful sense of satisfaction as you accomplish more and more every day. Your resistance to yourself is slowly fading away and disappearing completely. You know you are an honest adult and responsible person and you want to get your exciting life to progress on the road to success. You are leaving procrastination behind and will enjoy a sense of stronger emotions every day. From now onwards you are getting things done in a delightful manner and you are doing things on time. Every day your work is getting easier and easier and feeling more thrilling to accomplish."

I stuck to clear simple suggestions and personalized them to his current goals. As the script progressed, I incorporated words that depict emotions. Also, for greater effectiveness, I kept to the progressive form of the present tense in the script.

"You start by getting those little things out of the way. The kind of things that sidetrack you and divert your attention, just get them out of the way. You bring yourself up to date on the work that you do, whether they be errands, paperwork, projects or sales. You complete your tasks easily every day, comfortably, and you have the confidence in yourself as you approach a new task. You know you get the job done well, efficiently and properly. You have released the temptation to put off what needs to be done."

Upon awakening from hypnosis, Milton emerged with a dazed expression on his face. He had never talked of these experiences with anyone outside his family members before, and felt surprised he had divulged so much during the session. On my part, I felt happy. Having worked on the series of events that was associated with his subconscious mental expectancy would help to set the stage for breaking his established behavioral pattern later on.

He stayed quiet for a while and felt that he was now able to view his career losses more realistically. He seemed to be struggling with the "Why Me?" reaction. However, instead of grappling with the numbness and despair as he did in the past, he seemed to have chosen to search for meaning and inner wisdom. This was despite some lingering sadness.

Before Milton left the clinic he assured me that henceforth he would be moving towards a deeper dimension of reality. The pain of loss seemed to have brought him in closer touch with his own inner goodness.

Chapter Seven

Rite of Passage

> "As I always tell my clients: 'It doesn't matter whether you believe in reincarnation or not. The unconscious mind will almost always produce a past life story when invited in the right way.' Indeed I am sometimes inclined to think that even if the conscious mind is highly skeptical about the reality of past lives as historical memories, the unconscious is a true believer and is simply waiting to be asked."
>
> Roger Woolger, 1988

Milton returned to my clinic on 17 November. His ability to control his temper had improved and the tendency towards procrastination had lessened. He could get out of bed faster than before. Everything seemed to be positive after the first session.

During this visit, he surprised me by revealing the fact that he had dreamt about his past lives before. As a rule, past life dreams are uncommon and tend to appear only in those critical moments of our lives when the collective unconscious tries to remind us of what we have been through before. In Milton's case it was as if he saw his own past life played out like a movie in his dream.

In my experience, dreams are one of the commonest vehicles which the *inner self* uses to speak to our conscious minds. Milton was in National Service at that time. In the course of his military training he sustained a severe backache which lasted for five to six weeks till he found himself arching his back and became increasing hard to mobilize. Each time it would take him as long as ten minutes to relax his back muscles. The painful spasms became increasingly unbearable and he couldn't understand why.

One night he had an unmistakable past life dream with a feeling of half-conscious memories. In that vivid dream he was a Crusader in the Middle Ages. He joined a religious expedition launched in response to a call from leaders of the Byzantine Empire to fight against the Muslim Turks who had cut off the Church's access to Jerusalem. During the Crusade he was captured by the Muslim soldiers and was tortured in prison and his back muscles stabbed with a spear. Finally the soldiers took a spear and pierced him in the chest and killed him. The entry point of the chest wound was located exactly at the spot of his current birth mark. He woke up next morning and his pain had miraculously vanished. The aching feeling of the muscles was gone and the arching of the back disappeared.

Upon hearing his story, I decided that Milton was ready to undergo a formal past life regression with my assistance.

Following an induction, I used guided imagery of a magical garden with an approaching mist and then directed Milton to walk through the mist into a past life scene. Mental images promptly appeared the moment he stepped out of the mist.

"I am on a canoe in a river," he said. "I am alone, paddling towards a forest far away. I am a male, Red Indian in my twenties in this past life."

"Describe your clothing."

"There is deer skin around my waist. There is a little head band with a feather on my head. I am barefoot and paddling."

"Describe your surroundings to me."

"Not too sure if it is dawn or dusk. It's dim ... there is light ... more like a dusk. There is an orange tint in the sky overhanging the top of the forest. The forest is opening up on two sides and the river cuts through it. The river seems very long."

"How do you feel now?"

"Calm."

"What are your thoughts that accompany the calmness?"

"This is supposed to be a rite of passage ... I am supposed to find my totem."

I was taken aback. Not being familiar with the native Red Indian culture, I felt a little uncertain as to how best to continue. My understanding of a *rite of passage* is that the life of an individual in a society consists of a series of transitions from one age group or status to another.

Human beings are believed to evolve psychologically throughout their lives in chronological stages that progress through infancy, youth, midlife, and old age. This progression from one social position to the next is often accompanied by a culturally determined ceremony that publicly proclaims the individual's entry into a new status. The ceremony is specially designed to carry the individual from one phase of human experience to another. In all of these phases, trials and tribulations are present. The rite of passage is supposed to integrate the social and the sacred aspects of one's life.

I was pondering over what the meaning of "totem" was and what part it played in helping Milton to develop maturity at this stage of his life development. Intuitively, I felt it should refer to some object, animal or natural figure that serves as a distinctive mark or emblem representing the Red Indian clan. I decided to ask.

"What is that totem supposed to be?"

"Not sure. I will find out when I am there."

"Move on and tell me what happened next."

"I land by the right side of the bank. I go into the left channel of the river and I stop right at the bank where the river splits into two branches. I pull my canoe up the shore. I take my water pouch ... I walk right into the jungle."

"What happened next?"

"I am going through my mind what my totem is going to be. Is it a wolf? Or a bear? Or could it be just a normal piece of stone? So, all these images are running through my mind," he ruminated.

It was fascinating. I was vaguely aware of the fact that the ancient native Americans believed that animal spirits have inspirational power with lessons to impart. I later found out that the wolf's spirit is supposed to represent teaching skill, loyalty and independence. In shamanistic traditions the wolf is viewed as a powerful guide. The bear, on the other hand, symbolizes strength, introspection and self-knowledge.

"The sky is getting dark." Milton continued. "I set up a small little fireplace and a small clearing in the woods. I take out my rations and have some bites because I am hungry. I can't really fall asleep because I am excited as to what is coming. I am sitting there watching the fire and listening to the sound of the forest. "

"How do you feel as you sit there watching the fire?"

"Calm and curious."

"Move on and tell me what happened next?"

"I stand up, stretch myself, go into the jungle and stop. I take one step at a time. I need to accustom my eyes to the dark. Slowly I move. The jungle is pitch-black. My eyes slowly get accustomed to the darkness. I begin to see shades of black ... trees ... bushes ... and shadows. I am moving forward."

A sense of eagerness and anticipation was building up in Milton's voice.

"I have an expectant feeling that something may be happening. I can feel ... I can sense a big animal somewhere behind by my side and to the left watching me as I make my move forwards ... four-legged ..." (pause)

"Oh ... It is a giant wolf! His eyes pierce through the darkness. I can see the shape. I see the shining edges of the eyes. He isn't ferocious. He is just looking at me as if he is waiting ..."

"What emotions are you experiencing?"

"Excitement."

"What thoughts accompany the emotion?"

"This is the totem of my animal. This is my sign." His emotional energy seemed to have come up to a crescendo. The excitement in his voice sounded as if he was an actor winning an Oscar.

"The wolf is of pure silvery gray," he continued. "He's huge by any standard ... more mystical than real life. Under the pale moonlight I can see the fur is ruffled by the wind. I can hear the sound of the wind too ... whoo! ... it's loud! I am listening to the same sound as the wolf is listening to ... the whisper of the wind!"

I was amazed as well as excited at the detailed description that emerged from Milton during this life-changing moment.

"I take a step forward and the giant wolf takes a step forward too, looking at me in the eyes ... as if we recognize each other from many, many lives! We were friends before ... It's like seeing an old friend."

Milton suddenly broke into tears and went into catharsis. I did not expect this to happen, but allowed him to cry aloud for a while.

"The wolf howls ... the wolf howls," he sobbed. "We move forward towards each other. I kneel down and embrace the wolf. We embrace each other for a long time."

The energy remained strong. The critical moment when he and the wolf met was described as being "filled with racking emotions" after he emerged from the regression.

"What happened next?"

Fig. 12: "*As if we recognize each other from many, many lives!*"

"I am back to the clearing of the forest, at the fireplace. We are sitting looking at the fire together. The wolf asks me: Remember your ancient promise?"

"How did you reply?"

"What ancient promise? I asked back. (pause) ... It was to tread the path of no return, the wolf says. I know the path I take in this life – it's to serve humanity the way I want and never stop moving along the spiritual path."

The conversation was as intriguing as gazing at a crystal skull! I later learned that Native American tradition provides that each individual is connected with certain animal spirits that will accompany him through life, acting as guides. The predominant method of establishing a direct link to the spirit world and for healing is the *vision quest*. Often this involves isolation on a sacred mountain without food and water for days, and when the vision comes, it is a guide for life. Different animal guides enter into the individual's life depending on the direction he is heading and the task he needs to complete in the course of his journey. The wolf is apparently one such animal. The animal guide offers power and wisdom if and when the individual communicates with the wolf spirit. Some individuals innately know what their totem animal is and feel as if they are specially drawn to that particular animal energy. Subsequently when Milton was out of trance, he explained to me that "the wolf was the soul asking me to remember what I was here for". It was like getting in touch with his *Inner Self* again.

At this point, there was a sudden turn in the past life scene.

"The image of Bodhisattva (Guanyin) now appears in front of the fire ..." Milton suddenly said.

I was taken aback. Milton was not a Buddhist as far as I was aware. I later learned that he had been a regular practitioner of meditation and the image of Bodhisattva appeared quite frequently whenever he attained alpha state. This time he saw the Bodhisattva sitting next to the wolf opposite him. Together the three of them enjoyed the company of each other in a group meditation.

"I am reconnecting with my past," he continued. "This explains why I love the Red Indian culture so much. It also explains why certain vows are taken."

I was taken aback a second time.

"What vows have you taken?" I asked.

"To continue with my spiritual path and to never, never falter, despite the challenges ahead ... understanding that anger and procrastination are nothing but to foster the foundation to move forward ..."

It was a profound statement. I silently wondered how that beautiful line emerged. Milton seemed to read my mind telepathically.

"These messages just appeared in my mind. A voice is talking to me and whispering in my mind," he said.

"What other messages are getting through?" I asked.

"Those are perhaps the biggest challenges in my physical fabric now." His voice turned soft.

"What is your reaction to this?"

"Peace."

I intuitively realized that Milton had reached his peak experience again.

"Good ... stay with the experience and with the peace of the image of Bodhisattva in your mind," I said. "Freeze the moment of peace and calmness and stay with the moment of enlightenment."

Next I brought Milton back to the imagery of the healing garden from which he had stepped into his past life. "Stay in this garden now ... enjoy the place as it is where you want to mull over your anger. It is a beautiful, enchanting garden that gives you greater insight into yourself. I want you to think about what makes you angry in your daily life. Just feel yourself back in a situation where you have overreacted in an impulsive way and think about what you said to your family members or what was said to you, the tone of voice that was used, or the look, or maybe the situation was unjust or unfair ... or maybe you feel victimized in some way. Just let your subconscious mind bring forward such memory for you to work on. Feel those angry feelings inside you and make them stronger. Now locate those feelings in your body ... Where are they?"

"Left chest."

The presence of an associated physical location makes an emotion easier to process in hypnotherapy. I decided to use the opportunity to embody the emotion with physical attributes.

"Describe how you feel."

"Soaring ... energy moving non-stop."

"Can you give your anger a color?"

"Combination of red and black."

"Give it a shape."

"Like a whirlpool." His descriptive response made the hypnotic visualization much easier. As a rule, the more vivid and dramatic the image, the more effective the visualization will be because visualizations are also suggestions.

"Just focus on the shape and the color. Hear it ... see it ... and feel it for a moment. Feel the anger moving through your chest to your left shoulder, down the arm past the elbow and forearm into the wrist and hand and feel the anger there. Feel the shape, texture, color and the movements of the anger. It feels so bad that you just want to get rid of it. Feel your fingers wrap around the anger now. Then open your fingers now and blow away the anger. It has no place in you. You find amazing things happening to you as the anger is blown away, dissipating, dissolving away, disintegrating and dispersing ... You begin to feel very relieved. You are very calm now because you have gotten rid of the nasty feeling without destroying any relationships. A few moments ago you had all the anger inside you and now it is gone. What is left now is a wonderful feeling of calm and pride inside you. With all these comes peace of mind, and clarity of thought and vision. You will find you have no need to procrastinate anymore.

"From now on you have effective ways of dealing with your anger. In future when you need to diffuse your anger quickly you will feel your anger quickly move down to the fist and you let go. You are beginning to be a much calmer person now … more peaceful, more easy-going, more relaxed and happier. Each and every day you feel happier, calmer and more relaxed. You feel different inside. Other people will notice a difference in you."

Milton emerged from his hypnotic state looking refreshed and rejuvenated with a gleam in his eyes.

Several things had come to light in the course of this session. Milton had always loved dogs and had a long affiliation with wolves. Now he understood why. He loved to visit the National Parks in the United States while he was living there. At one time he was tracking in Middleton on a special track for wolves. He also tracked wolves in Yellowstone in the National Park. He had a strong affinity with the Grand Canyon. There was once he found himself strangely at ease while walking alongside the edge of the cliff without the slightest feeling of fear. Also, the past life explained why he had such a strong passion for canoeing. In fact he had been a canoeing instructor since young.

Chapter Eight

The Archetypal Beggar

"While re-experiencing past life events often brings about healing and change, the goal of looking beyond the veil of separation into the memories of the subconscious mind is to gather knowledge, wisdom, and understanding the deeper aspects of personality and character."

Mary Lee LaBay, 2004

Significant improvement took place in Milton soon after he went through the past life regression. While he could feel the anger coming on now and again, these emotions no longer escalated into outbursts. He was very happy that he could simply stop reacting to his angry feelings and everything could be brought under control at will.

The extent of procrastination had further improved. Whatever tasks he was confronted with for the day, he could comfortably finish them without delaying to the following day. He felt relieved. New project work no longer piled up, and he was focused on working hard to clear what had been lagging behind.

He came back on 22 November and asked for a further treatment for his procrastination.

Procrastination is a habit and in hypnotherapy positive affirmations and metaphors are often used to direct at the habit change. However, Milton's dramatic response in the previous session seemed to strongly suggest a past life origin to this habit. I agreed to perform another regression session and use an affect bridge to connect him with a past life.

With Milton relaxed on a reclining couch, I asked him to recall the last time when he was overwhelmed with the problem of putting off his responsibilities. As he got himself increasingly immersed with the event, I asked: "Is an emotion coming up? If so, let me know what it is."

"Lethargy," he replied promptly with his eyes remaining closed.

"Focus on the emotion of lethargy and amplify it several-fold ... now tell me what thought is associated with the emotion."

"Afraid ..." he says.

"What are you afraid of?"

"There is blackness in my mind now."

"Tell me the quality of the blackness."

"Dark ... some light is glowing on top. There are two different shades of darkness ..."

"Describe any emotions that are associated with this."

"Withholding ... withholding myself ..." Milton seemed to be struggling a little.

It appeared to be a moment when Milton needed some assistance. I decided to help him with a simple countdown from ten to one. When I reached the count of one, he was clearly back in a past life.

"I am in Ancient China, probably Ming Dynasty, and walking on a street, by myself. I am a boy, in my late teens, looking at the stall signs in the streets."

"Describe what you are wearing."

"I am wearing light brown clothing, a scarf and a rag around my head. There is some sort of a belt made of cloth at my waist. The shoes are made of cloth material. They are dark brown with stains. I am wearing a hat made of cloth."

"Tell me what is happening."

"I am crossing a stone bridge to the other side of the town. It is a residential area. I am just walking ... rows and rows of houses ... kids are lying around. I see an old lady by the door, sitting and talking. There are cobblestones on the street."

"What happened next?"

"I look forward and walk and turn right into an alley. It's a dead end. There are a few houses there facing each other. I turn back. There is an old lady on the left, smiling at me."

"Do you recognize her?"

"I don't know her." He paused. "She says to me: Come into the house. I contemplate. Should I do that? Then she says again: Come, come ...

"I am still standing at the corner of the street. I am not sure what makes me hesitate. Then other feelings come on." Milton sounded a little hesitant. "It's an inability to accept uncertainty. I am afraid to take the next step because I don't know what's going on ... don't know what may happen. It could be a gift; ... it could be a misgiving. Does she harbor any ill intention?"

"What did you decide then?"

"I decide to follow her ... thinking that nothing can really go wrong. So I go in."

"What did you see inside the house?" I asked.

"There is a table with a glass on the table ... white porcelain. She offers me a cup of water with that. The table is brown and square in shape ... a traditional bench. I sit down, thank her for the drink and take it. She asks: What are you looking for? You seem lost! I say I am just walking."

Silence followed. There was a long pause.

I felt a little puzzled by the silence. After a while, I asked: "What is happening?"

"The image of me has changed into a beggar."

I was a little surprised, but I decided to let him talk. I remembered from Jungian psychology that emotions translate directly into images. Hence exploring whatever image emerges provides an effective means of dealing with the patient's underlying emotions. This is unlike the situation in dream analysis in which the psychoanalyst perceives dream imagery as a façade that intentionally hides the dreamer's true meaning.

"My clothes are pretty rough. I am still in the house. The old lady is still there," he continued.

"What is the old lady's reaction when she sees you as a beggar?"

"That's probably the image she'd seen of me rather than the image I saw of myself earlier."

"What are your thoughts at this stage?"

"Somehow there's already an answer to why I stay where I am."

I was astonished. It seemed to be the supreme moment that both Milton and I had been waiting for.

"I am more accustomed to people using me ... handouts ... rather than creating a feature myself. As a beggar I wait for things to happen. I am surprised I didn't see myself this way. There is something deep down that I did not discover earlier. Probably there is a reason why I am directing my natural reaction this way ... in this life. I go the easy way out ... waiting for things to happen."

This was a moment of truth – another life-changing moment for Milton. This unexpected response that I got was better than what I had hoped for. Milton found the simple concept of beggar in his visualization deeply enlightening. It radiated a wonderful perception and this insight seemed to be the key to his recovery.

"What happened next?"

"I am back to this blackness ... contemplating what does this mean. The feeling of having the easy way out is very strong."

Fig. 13: "As a beggar, I wait for things to happen."

"What other thoughts are coming to your mind?"
"The word *move* appears in my mind."

"Focus on it and see if you can make out any meaning of the word."

"*Move* means moving not just my physical butt. I am actually too comfortable where I am ... way too comfortable ... from the physical sense and the spiritual sense, which relates to the procrastination. All the impulsive action I took, jumping into business, etc., was only a symptom that I need to move. I didn't know. It is actually a sign I need to move spiritually. I am stuck in a rut."

"Any thoughts on how to get out of this rut?"

"I need more practice ... more practice ... as in meditation, as in cultivation. I need to be focused. If I move, the rest will move naturally. Because of the inner core ... if I don't move, the outer will not move. Just way too comfortable where I am. I have to re-initiate the progress which I stopped for ten years to get back on my feet, to start moving."

"What is the message you are getting?"

"About all the spiritual cultivation that I am slacking ... Oh, I am back to the darkness again."

Milton was stuck with the visual darkness for a while and I waited for him to speak again.

"The glow on the blackness has become stronger, moving upwards. I am caught in this pure white light. It is shining white and my body is long and slender. Oh, I am healing ... I see long and slender hands and feet ..."

It was fascinating. The *white light* concept is something that we use in hypnosis quite often for healing purposes. In Section A, Gerald encountered a similar white light during his near-death experience. In Milton's case it had come to him spontaneously. In spirituality, the *white light* is often regarded as a Divine light, pertaining to the concept of protection and healing. The concept is easy to utilize in terms of visualization and is a powerful tool that the patient can use to help himself with.

"What emotions are coming through?"

"Peace ... I think I have the answer to all the problems with my procrastination."

It was a joyous moment for me as the therapist. I had managed to unravel enough of Milton's past for him to find the knot underlying his troubling symptom.

What I have learned in my training is that the subconscious mind works well with metaphors because of the latter's creative expression. I decided to deepen Milton's trance state and proceeded to weave his feeling of peace with the healing white light. Metaphors are known to enhance inner healing. Whether the white light truly represents a Divine light is unimportant. What matters is that the patient belief in the healing power of the white light can be mobilized to help himself.

"You will find your peace expanding in the presence of the white light," I said. "Feel this white light, the soothing white light, the protecting white light and the healing white light. As you feel the harmony within, you will feel the healing taking place. As the white light comes around you, you will feel calm, and so lovely that you are back to a stage where you feel enlightened."

The therapy ended on a wonderful note. Milton emerged from the session with a bright shining face. It was as if he had suddenly solved a puzzle that had troubled him for years.

Chapter Nine

Rage

> *"There is some powerful curative force in this (past life) realm, a force apparently much more effective than conventional therapy or modern medicines. The force includes remembering and reliving not just momentous traumatic events, but also the daily insults to our bodies, minds and egos."*
>
> Dr. Brian Weiss, MD, 1988

Milton returned two days later on 24 November. This was Day 10 of his therapy and I had come to understand him much better as an individual with a fascinating intellectual and spiritual background.

Milton had developed speed reading skills at the age of twelve and at one stage he could read as many as 54 books per week. "In the past we used to use library cards for borrowing books, and three books per card was allowed," he said. "Three books from my mum, three from my dad and three from my own card. The Chai Chee Public Library opened only on Monday, Wednesday and Friday. So every time the library opened I would go and change books ... nine, nine, and nine. For a good six months I was doing that. This is innate in me ... wanting to find more, and find more. Yet I am stuck. Financially I am doing well, but it does not mean anything. The spiritual part of me is still hollow."

Milton's wife was a Catholic. However, he himself belonged to the Eckankar faith, a religious order in which personal experience of the Light and Sound of God is the cornerstone. What fascinated me was that Milton had very interesting dreams. Sometimes he dreamt of himself as a Taoist priest and at other times dreamt of his life as a Franciscan monk in Scotland. He had once dreamt of himself studying in monasteries and in Chinese temples. All his life he had been very spiritually inclined. He personally felt that he needed just one final anchor to move on. Perhaps all those peaceful dream lives had created complacency in his attitude and could have unconsciously contributed to his symptom of procrastination.

After some discussion, we agreed to work further on his problem of anger management.

Anger is a human emotion that we all experience when things go wrong. Yet I wanted Milton to see that there is wisdom to be found in anger. With its sharp cutting edge, anger helps us to see what may be wrong and reminds us that something needs to change or be attended to. A key principle in hypnotherapy is to focus on people's strength and to amplify that strength. I therefore began with the premise that Milton's spirituality was a talent that I could draw upon as strength to help him find answers.

With this in mind, I got Milton to relax and recall a time when he felt frustrated by the sense of anger outbursts. As he drifted back to a previous event, I asked if any feelings were growing inside him.

"Rage," he replied.

As a therapist, I believe that suppressing anger and repressing rage have limited returns, unless we find constructive ways to channel these feelings into positive action. I preferred to make Milton see his anger as a cause for reflection and therefore used it as an affect bridge.

"Focus your mind on the rage to make it stronger, and I will help you to intensify it by counting from one to ten.

On reaching the count of ten, I found that Milton was already back in a past life.

"I see a dark shade of a coconut tree reaching out to the sea," he began. "I am alone. I'm a Malay boy, dark-skinned, short hair, about eight to twelve years old. There is a fringe on my forehead. I am barefoot, wearing shorts."

"What are you doing now?"

"I am standing by the beach in a small coastal fishing village. The village is nested in the bay. I see a couple of houses on stilts. They are classical Polynesian fishing houses. The boats are on the beaches, and sampans are lying around. There are kids playing by the water. There are ladies busy with their chores, washing clothes. The guys are out fishing."

"What are your emotions now?" I asked.

"Fear," he replied firmly.

"Fearful of what?"

"No idea of what. Just the word fear."

"Focus on the fear and see if there are any answers."

"I am an orphan. My parents went fishing and never returned. This has happened recently."

I sensed a clue. "What are your thoughts that go with this emotion of fear?" I asked immediately.

"I think my anger could probably have come from being left alone," he replied promptly.

"What is happening next?" I asked.

"I am looking around. I am at the stilt staircase of my own house. I am thinking whether I should join other children in their games by the beach. My uncle takes care of me now. There is a sense of sadness ... an overcast. I look around and decide to walk away from the other children who are playing on the other side of the beach. Nobody is staying at the other side. After reaching there I sit down at a log."

"What happened next?" I asked.

Suddenly the story turned intriguing.

"A figure appears as I am sitting," Milton said. "I know him. He is one of my Masters. He has a bearded face ... thick beard. His name is Tas. I look at him for guidance. He says it's okay. I take a step and dive into the water while he sits back and looks. I am diving and swimming. He is sitting at the rocks smiling at me."

"What happened after that?"

There was a pause. "There is this sense that my uncle is trying to take away all the money that my parents left behind," he continued with a tone of sadness. "I am back at the house but everything is empty. There is not much I can do. My uncle has left; I am alone in the house."

"Describe the house and your surroundings to me."

"There is one big living room. There is a door to the left where the kitchen is and a door to the right where I sleep in. It is a rectangular house on stilts."

"Ask your Master for advice regarding your plight."

"There is a certain cause-and-effect that you would not understand for now."

"How did you feel when you hear that?"

"How am I going to survive? I think the answer given by my Master is the key to the training for survival ... Learn to survive by yourself in your lifetime.

"So the story begins to unfold; I start to fish by myself, gathering fruits from the jungle behind the village. I am progressing pretty well. There is a sense of calmness. At this stage I am being fast-forwarded. I am two to three years older now. I am still at the same house. There is a fast-forwarded picture of myself fishing, getting food for myself, setting out and casting my net every day."

"As you do so, are any thoughts coming through?"

"I miss my parents and am crying in the house."

"Move on with your life and tell me what happened next."

"I am quietly leaving the village and do things on my own ... I am in teenage now. One day this sampan arrives with a young lady and her father at the other side of the village. They plan to set up a home there. Their old house in the other island was destroyed by tidal wave. The bay we are in ... is blocked by the mountain behind and so it is relatively calm. They thought it is a good place to set up home.

"I recognize this young lady is my wife in this current life! We courted and got married in that life too."

I later learned from Milton that he had a very novel-like courtship with his spouse in this present life. It started with a blind date. There was a bus stop outside the hospital where she was working and they agreed to meet there on their first date. "Chuh ... chuh ... chuh." Milton trotted down a flight of stairs leading to the main road. About 50 meters away from the bus stop in front of the hospital, he saw her there. Suddenly an overwhelming feeling came and he decided that she, and no one else, would be his wife. He had no second thoughts since, even though he had yet to see her face then!

"We go about our married life," Milton continued. "It is quite nice. We have a boy. He's a toddler, chubby little fellow. My life is pretty contented and happy."

"Move on to the next significant event."

"The entire village is wiped clean out by a huge tidal wave. I am sitting in the staircase crying. It is in debris. Nobody is staying on this island. I am extremely sad with the loss of my wife and son. I am crying away."

"What are your thoughts at this point?"

"Why again?" Milton said sadly.

"Ask your Master that same question and see what answer he gives you," I prompted as I sensed his sorrow.

Fig. 14: *"The tidal wave is coming!"*

"A loss in this life does not mean a loss in Eternity. You will meet them again ... The boy I lost is my second son in this life. It explains why I am so fearful of losing my children in this life."

"Any other insights coming through?"

"Everything in this world is physical. Nothing will stay the same. Rebuild and carry on, he said."

There was another moment of silence, and I decided it was time to guide Milton to the next significant event.

"I am on a train in India," he began again.

"Where are you heading to?"

"I have no idea. The train is full of people. I am moving to the center of the subcontinent. I am in my late twenties, travelling by myself. The train is cutting through forest and fields. The journey seems endless at this point."

"What are your emotions at this stage?" I asked.

"Expectant of things going to happen ... I feel a new life is coming."

"What happened next?"

"I found myself a seat by the window looking out. The sun's setting. It's another three hours before I arrive.

"I am at the station now ... leaving the train ... it's full of people. I have a suitcase. I can't make out the station's name. I am supposed to go to the temple ... to study under the Head Monk. He is bald, pretty old, a bit fat, on the plump side, and wearing a white half-body robe."

It sounded like a pilgrimage, and I listened attentively for more details.

"I'm inside a temple now. My dress-up is like his."

"What happens next?"

"I study the Hindu scriptures. The regime is strict."

"How did you adapt to it?"

"I am happy to be studying the scriptures, but I am playful too. I have been caned many times on the head for not paying attention, but I can sense the teacher likes me. The sense of understanding of the scriptures is there, but for prolonged use this understanding does not bring about enlightenment. It brings a different meaning for life but not enlightenment. I was contemplating should I turn into a *Samsara* or should I stay in the temple and become a priest."

I was taken aback. As far as I was aware, *Samsara* is a Sanskrit word which literary means "to flow on" and pass through states of existence. The term is often used in the context of a cycle of repeated birth, death and reincarnation. In this case, I took it that Milton meant his desire to perpetually wander in his life to search for the truth. It was the first time I had heard this word coming from a patient. What came to light subsequently after the session was that Milton had studied the entire Gita[20] when he was only twenty-two years old in his current life.

"What was your decision?"

"The search for truth is so strong. If I stay with the temple it will not allow me to enlighten, and I know it.

"I walk into the jungle to begin a life of hardship, fasting and meditation. I can project my soul to anywhere but I can not find enlightenment. I die in that life in the jungle, not reaching my goal either."

"How old were you when you die?"

"At around forty-five to fifty years."

"Who else was with you when you died?"

"I am alone when I die. The thought before I die: So what with this power. It does not really bring enlightenment. I stop breathing. I am looking at my body downwards ... Still at the jungle. As I am leaving my body, I come to this whiteness ... just plain white."

---

[20] Gita is the short form of Bhagavad Gita, a 700-verse Hindu scripture written in Sanskrit. It contains a conversation between a prince and his guide on a variety of philosophical issues.

"Go to the spirit realm."

"I am there now ... in the spirit realm. I am speaking to my spirit guide. He is my old Master in my previous life."

"Ask him what is the lesson you are supposed to learn."

"He says: You already knew, and knew long ago."

"How did you feel?"

"I feel consoled, a sense of recognition and understanding."

"Ask your spirit guide how is the lesson related to your present life issues?"

"Anxiety coming from the loss of my son ... Procrastination; you already know what is going on. You are not working on an anxiety that you cannot handle ..."

In my experience with patients under hypnosis, there is something special about the experience of being in the spirit realm. The trance state allows for an enhanced sense of personal control and greater flexibility in responding to situations. The unconscious processes helped Milton to mobilize more effective information processing and reflexive positive responses. This facilitated a change in the quality and direction of his thinking.

"Procrastination in spiritual development was due to the fact I have tried everything. I thought trying again will not help; doing it all over again will not help," Milton continued.

"Ask your Master what is likely to be of help."

"Discipline," he responded firmly.

"What is the best way to achieve this discipline in your current life?"

"Just do it ... Stop feeling ... Stop thinking. Just do it. It is the mental thought and emotion that holds me back. So what if I have done it before!"

At this point Milton was ready to leave the spirit realm and I told him that I had brought him to a place of healing. "What do you see?" I asked.

"I see wine on the table. Room is all white. Another spirit Master is standing on my right. He is shining through my body with light."

After guiding him through a short healing imagery, I directed Milton back to the here and now. He opened his eyes and exclaimed in excitement: "More answers ... and very interesting!"

Many a time I have noticed that no matter what issues the patient brings to the therapist, he unsuspectingly brings his own answers and solutions together. Such was the case with Milton. Much of my effort had really been spent in helping him to clear the psychological noise that had prevented him from harmonizing his life with himself.

"Procrastination is the manifestation of my inability to act in my Inner Self, because of my attitude of today: *Been there, done that. I don't have a result; so why am I doing it again? So just wait and see,*" he explained.

Milton had now established full clarity with regards to his issues. He understood what he had lost in his past life, and the crises he experienced as a result of the pain and suffering created. However, his losses were also transformative. After knowing himself better through the regression therapy, he appeared strengthened by his losses and was no longer being blindly driven by a gale wind.

Of note, Milton's past life events had strong spiritual overtones. His past life complexes were dominated by metaphors and archetypes while the stories brought forth mythic patterns and religious motifs which in turn served as vehicles for accelerated healing. After the session ended, Milton brought to light certain spiritual aspects of himself, including how he used to strengthen himself spiritually through fasting.

"This spiritual part of my past life explains why I can go fasting any time, whenever I feel like it. Usually I do it on a Friday, and for twenty-four to forty-eight hours I don't eat. Fasting is a part of mind training to focus myself."

I was astounded.

This session turned out to be the last therapy session I had with Milton. Five days later he called to thank me for what I had done. He reported a huge improvement in his procrastination and anger management. What he had previously perceived as an obstacle in his life had turned out to be a catalyst for spiritual growth. He indicated that it was time he moved on.

I have always found the patient's desire to move on in life as being a reliable indication of his inner transformation. Moving on implies previous stagnancy of the passage of time; but now things will never be the same again for Milton.

Section C

Search and Struggle

Chapter Ten

Misty Memory

"Looking at one's biography in the light of one's past lives is much like looking at an entire landscape – horizon, sky, hills, fields, and flowers – as opposed to looking at one small patch of flowers narrowly focused through a camera lens."

Barbara Findeisen, 1992

In inner healing, the search for the origin of sickness goes further back than the pathophysiology on which Medicine focuses. In fact it goes back to the emotional, psychological and spiritual levels. In so doing, one seeks answers to questions surrounding the circumstances of one's life: *Why me? Why now? Why in this manner?* This transcends the mechanistic cause-and-effect model that focuses on a specific event or a set of contributory factors that sensitized the individual to the disturbance in physiological homeostasis.

The next few chapters describe a patient's continual struggle in her search for meaning in her life. At the age of forty-three Clarissa had experienced many years of working as a preschool educator, but more recently she was troubled by her groping for life directions. She was looking forward to a career change. Deep within, she had been experiencing an inner yearning that she wasn't who she thought she was, and that there was brightness and hope ahead of her. In recent months she had been developing an increasing interest in healing practices and was beginning to feel a calling to engage in therapy work. However, her spiritual growth had not come as a one-shot awakening, but as a journey of stages in which the hidden self was unveiled stepwise in an evolutionary process. In fact she came to me with a conglomeration of seemingly unrelated symptoms successively one after another, presenting themselves over weeks and months.

Clarissa had always struck me as a unique and highly hypnotizable patient. She differed markedly from many other patients in that she could become deeply absorbed in the therapy experiences at a very rapid rate. Highly imaginative, she could respond to suggestions across situations and process information quickly under trance. She also showed a very high theta wave pattern on her EEG[21] tracings. Furthermore she tended to be fantasy-prone during regression and able to see imagined things as real. Interestingly, in my preliminary conversation with her, she divulged that she had been expending some of her time interacting with her spirit guides and guardian angels. During therapy sessions, she was able to experience profound alterations in consciousness and trance states with no special prompting. Her special talents had allowed me to utilize her imaginative abilities to good advantage in my hypnotherapy sessions with her.

On 18 April 2011 Clarissa suddenly got in touch with me with a problem of functional memory loss. She complained of difficulty recalling day-to-day events and described herself as seemingly "shutting off" all her memory. Sometimes she felt as if all her memory capacity would get "washed out" after one week. This started to bother her when her husband noticed that she had been unable to recall the dinner outings they recently had together, the restaurants they frequented and the people they met. The last dinner date she had with her husband was barely a fortnight back, and to her dismay she was totally unable to remember the details

---

[21] EEG is abbreviation for electroencephalogram, a recording of electrical activity on the scalp that measures the voltage changes in the nerve cells of the brain.

of that treasured evening. She was concerned that the memory impairment had begun to impact on her life.

"At the present moment I have a good time with my family, have dinner, have celebration with my parents, go to this place and do everything we want," said Clarissa. "Then after that, just tomorrow or one week later, I am totally washed out with my memory and my husband gets very frustrated with me.

"Because I use a lot of my brain and I have so much to remember, I have no more residual capacity. So I make this decision that I am going to shut off my memory, and I don't know if this is the problem that is affecting me."

I was perplexed. "You mean you are actively shutting out your memory?"

"Yes," she replied. "I think I am shutting out, which means to say that I do not want to register everything in my mind. It is to free up my memory space. It's because in my lower secondary schooldays I had a lot to study and I had to study the smart way. I am not the academic type of person. Then up to a point when my memory bank is filled up, I cannot take in anymore. Then I make a decision to let go and tell myself I am not going to remember anything.

"I don't know whether that impacts on my performance. Then at one time my friend exclaimed: Clarissa, how is it that you cannot remember? We had such fun in school! We go for dinner here and had such great fun! When I told her that I really cannot recall, she was very disappointed with me.

"Before I gave birth to my first child, I used to have very good memory in my work and remembering data, numbers and information. After I gave birth to my girl, my memory was totally wiped off, but one year later it came back. So for that one year I was very handicapped and my boss even asked me to resign. I was so inefficient and I had to start all over again. In the second year the memory started coming back but I am already losing half of my memory now. I cannot keep going like this from bad to worse. Something is blocking. I do something and I don't what is it for … but I know that the more spiritual I go, the more challenges there are and the more obstacles I face."

It was a long and perplexing story. I asked about her childhood and she had not experienced any traumatic events. She also felt there was no reason to suspect an early onset of dementia. However, one thing was clear in her mind. Whatever struggle she was going through, she saw it as an opportunity for spiritual growth and a challenge to turn the ordinary into the extraordinary. After some discussion, we decided that a past life regression might help her.

After Clarissa had settled down comfortably on the reclining couch, I turned on some relaxing music. Despite her being a highly hypnotizable subject, relaxing music remained useful in deepening her hypnotic state quickly.

Within thirty seconds Clarissa was in a trance state and experienced a strong emotion of anger associated with her loss of memory. Using anger as an affect bridge, she was connected with a couple of interesting past lives.

In the first past life, she saw herself as a girl about eighteen years of age in a castle in Russia. She was a daughter of a political minister. She saw herself meeting and falling in love with a 26-year-old man. The man was a soldier but was forcibly taken away to fight in a war after their romance was discovered.

"How did you fall in love with him?"

"We met in the garden by chance. He is not supposed to be there. It is a forbidden garden, which is only for the royals."

"What happened after you fell in love?"

"We went on secret dates. We were found out and we were separated. He was taken away and made to go to fight the war. He did not have a chance to say anything to me before he left and he never came back."

"How did you feel when he never came back?"

"He was killed. I did not cry. I didn't feel anything because I had numbed my emotions. When he was taken away he turned back and looked at me exactly the same as the first time he looked at me."

"Describe your emotions when you know he died in the war."

"No feelings ... numb. I did not want to feel. If I feel I would be very sad. I felt I was betrayed."

"What happened next, now that the person you love did not come back?"

"I moved on."

"What is the lesson you learned in this lifetime?"

"I learned to love myself."

I got as far as this point before sensing some painful memories that Clarissa did not want to recall. So I moved her on to another past life.

At the second past life, Clarissa appeared as a man. "I was a brave warrior put behind the bars," she started. Occasionally I do encounter mild bewilderment in some patients who saw themselves in the opposite gender in a different life. This is almost never a problem if they have been prepared beforehand. It helps to explain that the male and the female are actually divided halves of one primordial being, and each half looks to the other for its completeness. What we pursue at the level of the Higher Self during regression therapy is a sense of our own completion. Often this sense of wholeness comes about when the masculine and feminine sides of our psyche get united.

"I was imprisoned," she continued. "They wanted some information and I refused to give it. I was tortured until I lost my memory, half of my memory."

Fig.15: "*They wanted some information and I refused to give it.*"

"Which country were you in?"

"Romania. They tortured me in a cell because they wanted information from me. I lost my memory."

"How old were you when you were tortured?"

"Twenty-eight years of age. They tortured me until I went unconscious and my body was thrown into a jungle. There were animals around."

"How did you deal with the animals?

"They became my friends."

"What happened next?

""Half of my memory is gone. I cannot remember."

"What happened after you made friends with the animals in the jungle?"

"I just lived my life with them ... till the day I died."

At this point Clarissa started crying.

"What happened?" I asked.

"I was in the jungle and saw someone die. I bent down to look at the body. Then somebody shot me."

"Who shot you?"

"He was a soldier, a Romanian soldier. I was wanted. They found me in the jungle and tried to shoot me to death.

"What happened next?"

"I stayed alive and they brought me back to the cell."

"What happened after they brought you back to the cell?"

"I was tortured more."

"Did you regain your memory?"

"I refused to speak."

"Why did they torture you?"

"They wanted information. It was information about the country, I could not give to them. I decided to erase it from my memory so that they cannot have it."

"What happened when they continued to torture you? Did you persist or did you give up?"

"They tortured me till I died because I had no information to give. I eventually died in the cell. I was fifty-eight when I died."

"How did you feel then?"

"I felt injustice."

"What are your thoughts in relation to the injustice?"

"I had to die because of information. I had to sacrifice myself because of information. I was not willing to leave the body. They buried me. I imprisoned myself in the body. I don't want to go anywhere. I am tired. I wish to stay still. I don't have to answer to people. I don't have to do anything and don't wish to go anywhere. I like it this way."

There was a lot of reluctance for the soul to leave the body at the death point. Eventually when it did leave, I directed the soul to the spirit realm to communicate with her spirit guide. This is a technique that I often employ in past life therapy. Her death point was the locus of accumulation of a lot of negative thoughts, feelings and sensations of that life. Work needed to be done to release and reverse the psychic residues. As a spiritual exercise, a dialogue with a spirit guide has the benefit of removing fear of death and leads to some form of spiritual empowerment. Psychically the process gives a sense of immortality to the patient while allowing her to obtain enlightenment from beings more spiritually evolved than herself. As a psychotherapy technique, it helps to provide room for creativity and problem-solving ability.

"Ask your spirit guide what is the lesson you are supposed to learn from this past life?"

After a minute of silence, Clarissa went into catharsis and was sobbing away.

"The spirit guide told me not to be disheartened. Move on in life. Just move on ... no matter what happens don't be disheartened."

"Ask your guide why did you have to lose your memory in this past life?"

"It was because I did not want to move on. It is very painful to move on. Very, very painful. (crying) The pain is beyond description."

"What makes it so painful to move on?"

"It's being wrong all the time. I did not have a chance or opportunity to explain because I can't. I am in a situation in which I cannot explain. I just have to sacrifice myself and my life. I died for people ... for the bigger picture. I have no life ... no life. (crying) I died for the people ... for the country. (crying) I cannot betray them or they would die. Either I die or so many other people would die." (crying)

"So you are the martyr for the country?"

"I don't want the job. I hate to be a martyr," she said while her emotions were mounting.

"I hate to be the chosen one. I don't want to be the chosen one. I don't want to sacrifice. I hate my job. I don't have life. It is all for the people, all for the country ... sucks ... sucks. I hate them for choosing me and doing what they did to me. I hate them." She cried even louder.

"Ask your spirit guide why did they choose you?"

"They say I am the most powerful. They say I can do the job. I hate to do it. They say I fit into the job. For what? Why am I doing this? So what if I fit the job? So what? ... So what? What are they doing?"

Clarissa's voice was teeming with anger. The emotional release was rising up to a crescendo and became a full outburst.

"Why have I to be the one? I have sacrificed myself. (crying) Why do I have to sacrifice myself for the country? It's so hard. I have to sacrifice myself. Why do I have to sacrifice myself? For what? What spirituality is this? ... sucks ... sucks ... (crying) I lost my loved ones. Why? I do not want to be the one. Please leave me alone ... I don't want. (crying) I cannot take this anymore. Help me! (crying loudly and emotionally) Why? I want a normal life. I don't want this anymore. Please choose somebody else. Leave me alone ... leave me alone. I don't want. Give me a chance. Let me go. I cannot take it anymore. (crying) Help me ..."

Clarissa had reached the peak of the catharsis. I decided that it was time to get her into a healing phase. I told her to take a deep breath and the crying stopped momentarily.

One of the lessons I learned from my training is that all living things in nature have within them the incredible capacity to heal, be they plants or animals. For instance, the feel of a soft breeze blowing away stress, bringing strength and a sense of wellbeing can be a very soothing experience. Visualizing a brisk wind that blows away disease is often very invigorating. Water too can be healing. This could be figuratively swimming in a magic pool or immersing oneself in some sort of healing water. At this juncture, I improvised a healing script:

"You are now in a place of healing. Slowly, you find yourself walk into a healing garden with tall trees and green shrubs on both sides. You smell the sweet scent of the flowers and hear the humming sound of insects in the background. You sit down by a rock to enjoy the magical healing power of the environment. Soon you find yourself calming down and relaxed."

While still in trance Clarissa had stopped crying.

"Take another deep breath slowly and see yourself sitting back and relax. Feel the gentle touch of the breeze blowing at your face, blowing away your sadness. Listen to the sound of rustling leaves and the birds chirping in the air. Enjoy the pleasant, cool environment while in front you see a pond with fish swimming peacefully in the water ... once in a while you see a fish popping out above the water surface to catch an unwary insect and then dive down again to join its companions. As you get close to the pond, you sit down and enjoy the peace and quiet of the garden."

The occasional sob had disappeared and Clarissa was much calmer now.

"It's wonderful," I continued. "You are feeling much better now. Take another deep breath slowly. Healing is taking place within you. Spirit guides have come and gone from this place before, and many others have come here to find their healing. While you are still in front of the pond, you pick up a pebble and throw it into the center of the pond, causing ripples to form in concentric circles of increasing diameter spreading to the periphery. At the same time feel the ripples of healing energy originating from the core of your body spreading to your periphery. You feel so much better now. When you are fully healed I will bring you back to the here and now ..."

Clarissa emerged from the guided imagery feeling refreshed and wonderful. As she mopped her tears, I saw her shining eyes. She appeared to have acquired new insights into herself.

"Oh! Thank you so much. I am fine really," she said as the nurse chaperone helped her to get down from the couch. Turning to me with a gleam in her eye she said: "I can relate that story with this lifetime."

"Can you?" I was delighted.

"Yes," she said emphatically. "Those stories were the past. In this lifetime I have a wonderful husband, beautiful kids and very supportive people in my family. They are all very well. Just now in the healing session the message I get is that I will be protected; not like in the past where I had to sacrifice myself. This time round whatever I do I will be protected and guided."

"Hmm, I see," I said.

"So I recalled when I was studying in Secondary 2, I had this dream that I saw this cave I was in." She started to tell a story.

I was again delighted, because the dream is a vehicle with which the soul speaks to our consciousness. Our dreams are unique to ourselves and they are connected to our individual reality. I encouraged her to elaborate.

"Suddenly there was a light and a spiritual being appeared in front of me. The spiritual being told me to do what I am supposed to do, to lead my life well and do good deeds; everything will be provided and I will be taken care of. So those are the things that I can actually relate to."

In our mundane lives we often find it difficult to believe that we are someone special. Yet most of our spiritual traditions teach us the opposite – that we are indeed someone special and possess a spark of the divine within us. Time and again this spark of hidden riches in our inner life gets woven into our dreams.

"I forgot about this dream for about ten years or so and I have been doing things that I am supposed to do. Even if it means I have to defy people to do it, I have to do it. Yes, I have been leading my life that way. And then, there's help along the way. I have a good family, friends and support. So there are a few people who tell me that what I have in this lifetime is what I have reaped in my past life; that I have done something to benefit this lifetime."

I understood what Clarissa was referring to when she talked about defiance. As a child she studied in a Convent School in Malaysia. Although she was brought up in a Catholic family she could not relate with the religious doctrines taught in the catechism classes in school. She defied the nuns in the school and did not see eye to eye with the parish priests. Despite all this, she remained a spiritually inclined person.

"Does the memory loss make sense?" I steered the subject away slightly.

"It was so clear that I shut it off … because the only way is to shut. And if I do not shut, they'll torture me until I reveal the information. It is the patriotic style … I also don't know why. I think it is political. That is why in this lifetime I do not like politics.

"My father happened to be a politician for a greater part of his lifetime. He is a great man, and is everything – he is black and he is white. He is the police and he is also the gang. He has support at that level from both sides. He is a genius, like Albert Einstein … and because of his political life, that brings him up and also brings him down. He protects us, his wife and children, by not shining us in front. We are always at the back stage. In a way we are protected, but the impact is still there. So, I didn't like it.

"And that is why every time I do healing, many people said to me: Clarissa you are very unusual. People are either angry or sad, but you are always in pain, intense pain. So today when you went through the whole thing and then the word 'pain' came out. The two things are very real – the memory and the pain."

Her profoundness impressed me. The theme word "pain" seemed to have triggered off a series of new insights while she was under hypnosis.

"And I am very much into spiritual work. My husband even said that I am addicted to spiritual stuff, which is scary. I go all the way because the inside here is telling me that I need to clear myself as much as possible. So I have the feeling sometimes that I just want to go high up into a mountain cave, meditate there and not come back."

It was a long session, and it ended with Clarissa in high spirits. I checked with her a month after the therapy, and she confirmed she was rid of the memory loss problem.

Chapter Eleven

Fear of Success

"Individuals consciously or unconsciously program their lives. The behavior in each life determines in some way the experience of the next. We make our own destiny and create our own environment. We purposefully choose parents, life settings, and lessons to be learned in each lifetime, all the events and relationships that are necessary for our growth and development."

Hazel Denning, 1992

Six months later Clarissa returned to my clinic. It was in the afternoon of 25 October 2011. While she confirmed that she remained free of the problem of memory loss, she was now bothered by a new symptom.

Clarissa was then in a career transition and wanted badly to move on to another job. However, she began experiencing an unexplainable anxiety, characterized by an irrational fear of success. The symptom sounded bizarre. However, she repeatedly said that she sensed an irrepressible fear to succeed in her next endeavor.

After some discussion, we decided that there may be other embedded past life issues that needed to be unraveled.

One of the unique factors of my therapy sessions with Clarissa was that she used metaphors extensively to describe her regressed scenes. These metaphors tend to have a profound impact in that they communicate powerful messages that can be easily understood and remembered. Such messages also tend to teach, guide and inspire whoever listens to them.

"Take three deep breaths ... Concentrate on your fear of success ..." I began.

Within seconds the intensity of her emotion gained strength.

"I sense a lot of fear," she said.

"Use this fear to connect yourself with an event in the past life during which you experienced the emotion in the same way."

Surprisingly this was all I needed to say to guide her into a past life.

"I see a young girl. Daddy holding hands, walking around in an amusement park. She is a very happy young girl, cheerful, smiling all the time."

"What is she doing?"

"She is riding a horse on a merry-go-round in an amusement park. Her daddy is watching. Shortly afterwards her mum comes. They look like a happy family."

"What happened next?"

"A dark storm came and destroyed the whole place, broke up the family, brought the dark clouds and sent the girl up to the sky. She was calling for Mummy and Daddy down below."

Things sounded weird. However, I soon realized that the reconstruction of Clarissa's past life story depended very little on imagery but heavily on her free flow of feelings and the information that came through as spontaneous thoughts.

"What happened to her in the dark cloud up there?"

"She's alone, and sad. There are dark clouds around her ... She has been with the dark clouds for a very long time. She never smiles any more. She misses her parents. She can see her parents down there. She cannot go there. She was six years old then ... she was me!"

It sounded dark!

Fig. 16: "A happy young girl, cheerful, smiling all the time."

"What stops her from going there?

"She is in a place where I cannot see anything. It is an empty space and she just feels confined in the empty space that has nothing to block her from going out. But she simply cannot go out. Surrounding her are dark energies. She is caged there.

"Her parents are very wealthy, and a happy family, loving couple. Her father trades her with the condition that if they release her he will give all his possessions to them to exchange for the girl. That happens and the girl returns to the family. They become poor."

"Who did the father give his possessions to?"

"The dark clouds," she said unhesitatingly. "There is no identification of any person."

It sounded like a description of Pluto's palace!

"Where is the girl now?"

"Back with the family, feeling very sad, because the parents are sad. They are now struggling for proper meals. It was never like that before."

"What happened after that?"

"The girl grows up. The parents pass away. Her dress is torn and re-sewn, dirty. She is twenty-eight years old now and looks poor."

"What is she doing now?"

"Looking up in the sky and wondering ... no thoughts ... no questions. She lives day by day all by herself ... no communication ... no friends."

"What happened next?"

"A guy came along and wanted to be her friend. She rejected him. She kept to herself and she remained contented in this way till she died."

"How did she die?"

"She died old, and frail. No one at the deathbed ... all alone. She wanted it that way."

"Has she left her body now?"

"Yes. She is wandering in the space up there in the sky. She is happy wandering."

Being at the death point, I directed her to go to the spirit realm.

"What did you see?" I asked.

"Some kind of a judge .... she is kneeling down ... not clear. There are three of them in front of her." Her description was consistent with that of spirit guides.

"It looks like an emperor's seat and one of them is sitting on it. She is bowing to them."

"What did the three of them say to her?"

"They ask her: Why are you torturing yourself in that manner? She replies she is happier that way, so that she would not recall the past. They ask her if she wants to be like this all the time and she says yes. They then ask her why? She says so she can forget the past. They ask her if she is sure that is the decision, and she says yes."

"Ask her what is her purpose of living a life like that?"

"Her life purpose is to have a happy family and to be happy but she lost all of it. So she has not found any meaning since then. She wanted to be with her Mummy and Daddy every day and be happy the way they used to be. However, Daddy was very sad because he lost all the money. Mummy was affected and they began to neglect her. There was no communication and not much interaction. They were feeling sad and she was affected. And she asked: Is money that great? Her daddy told her yes. Her daddy told her the root of whatever she receives: love, joy, happiness, fun ... everything, is money.

"She has decided that in order not to feel the pain anymore she is going to remove the root of the cause, which is money. She is telling herself she could live without money and she is equally happy. She did not want history to repeat itself."

"So what is the life lesson here that is associated with your fear of success and money?"

"I am happy without money, however, it is my entitlement that I receive more than what I am having now. It is my birthright. I need to receive it."

"Then why do you fear success?"

"It relates to money. Lots of money does not give you happiness ... In my current life I have been doing without money and I am still happy, and that was what the girl said. And the message is: Whatever it is, it (money) is my birthright and I need to claim it back."

"So, you found the answer to your own fear then?"

Clarissa nodded her head in trance.

"In a moment I will bring you away from the spirit realm to a place of healing where you can reflect over your sense of love and principles of living. At the count of three, tell me what do you see; one, two and three ..."

"A white mist ... I am seeing images of Guanyin."

Given Clarissa's spiritual background this imagery did not come as a surprise. What immediately came to mind is that the image of Guanyin, often known as the Bodhisattva of Compassion by East Asian Buddhists, could be an ideal theme for guided healing.

"Focus on the image of Guanyin (观音) ... the image of love and compassion. Feel the emotions of mercy and kindness, and this is where you will obtain your inspiration to move forward in life. *Guan* (观) means "to observe and watch" and *Yin* (音) means "sound", especially the sounds of those who suffer. As you concentrate on the image of Guanyin, you watch for and respond to the people in the world who need help. As long as you are kind and have love in your heart, you will reach out with your hand to heal others in the same way as Guanyin is sending her hands out to heal you. As you do so, immerse yourself totally in the healing environment."

Suddenly emotions were coming on and Clarissa began to move her body.

"Tell me what is happening," I said.

"I sense healing and forgiveness. There is healing on my financial concerns and relationships."

"Good. Just stay with the experience and continue to immerse in the healing energy."

Suddenly I noticed changes in Clarissa's facial expression.

"Do you have an experience to share?" I asked.

"A *white light* is coming into my body," she said softly.

"Very good. Allow the white light to come into your body, because the white light has healing properties."

In the course of my training I had learned to work with whatever imagery or feelings that emerge from the patient, and the approach had consistently worked well.

"Look at the white light in front of you ... you'll see it as a white glowing ball, slowly enlarging in diameter ... getting brighter and brighter coming near you. It is slowly entering your body and healing you of all emotional wounds that have been inflicted in the past. It is getting bigger and bigger ... till it occupies your entire body ... permeating all cells and tissues. And now your whole body is filled with the white light ... glowing away. It's so beautiful with this white light inside you. Let it stay for a while to purify your consciousness ... In a moment when the healing is complete you will see this white light slowly leaving your body, getting smaller and condensed. Slowly leaving your body, the white light is rising above you ... floating away, getting higher and higher until it fades into the distance. Now your healing is complete and you are feeling wonderful in every way."

Clarissa emerged from the session feeling exuberant and high in energy. I could sense that eagerness and exhilaration was overflowing. It felt as if she would just get up and walk straight into her next business venture!

Chapter Twelve

Fear of Public Speaking

"Sometimes one past life therapy session is enough to help a patient gain insight and make a big turn-around in his or her life."

Dr. Norman Shealy, MD, PhD

Another month passed and Clarissa returned. She no longer harbored any fear of success and was working towards getting a new job. However, what deterred her was another new problem. Strangely she now experienced a difficulty with communication.

It was the afternoon of 25 November 2011. Clarissa looked perplexed with herself.

"Somehow, I don't like to talk to people, and I have a problem with public speaking. I cannot deliver a structured speech in front of an audience, although informal interaction with people is not a problem. I would like to have a therapy session."

After she relaxed on the couch, I helped her to define her symptom in more detail. Slowly it became clearer that it was the frustration that she had to grapple with, whenever she found herself blocked in her thoughts and words. I pondered for a moment and decided that this emotion might provide the needed associative bridge to the initial sensitizing event.

"Concentrate on your feeling of frustration revolving around fear of public speaking ... and slowly, tell me what is happening."

Again, this single sentence directed Clarissa all the way into a past life.

"I see a boy writing at a desk," she began. "He is a smart intelligent boy coming from a poor background."

"What is he writing about?"

"About life. He is a thirteen-year-old boy giving away secrets about life. He is doing it discreetly."

"What is the reason for doing it discreetly?"

"The era does not allow such publications."

"Which era is it?"

"Fifteenth century."

"So he wants to share about his life experiences with the world?"

"No. He wants to tell how human beings are supposed to lead their life in the world. He wants to share the secret of living on earth in the peaceful, harmonious and prosperous manner, without the need for a lot of struggle, including pain, which can be eliminated. However, nobody believes him."

I learned later from Clarissa that this scene of a very bright young boy happily writing on a carton box by the desk was the only scene that she could clearly visualize during the entire regression. The subsequent past life story that followed this scene came spontaneously as *thoughts* rather than images. The remaining story was emerging as a series of spontaneous thoughts that flowed seamlessly and revolving around the video-like imagery of the boy at the writing desk for the rest of the session. It sounded almost as if she was *channeling*.

Channeling is a term that is often used to describe the esoteric process of receiving messages or inspiration from a divine source. By sensing which thoughts come from an external source, these thoughts are passed on as messages with much clarity. "The story just comes up spontaneously by itself ... just here, just the feeling, and I just say it out ... no need to even go through my mind," she remarked.

"Do you know the boy in your current life?"

"I was the boy," she said unhesitatingly.

"Tell me how you feel about what you are writing."

"Frustrated, hopeless, and unjust."

"What are the thoughts that go with these feelings?

"Disappointment with human beings and human nature. I am very disappointed that they make his life so difficult. Life is not supposed to be that difficult. They do not believe him. They make his life so difficult. I am angry with humans and with all the people who are so foolish. They like to live in suffering. They look for more and more suffering and they complain about it. I feel a deep sense of waste. All the information is not being heard nor used. All the secrets are there but nobody is using it. Such a waste ... very disappointed. I have to live with that feeling. What else can I do? It's their choice!"

"What is happening next? Are you still writing?"

"He spends most of his time writing and writing. He writes lots and lots of things. He calls it Divine Secret."

"What do you see in this situation as being related to your problem in your current life?"

"I cannot express because I am not allowed to express. It is not right to express. It is not acceptable."

"Is there a lesson you can learn from this?"

"In order to survive and live I have to shut up. I cannot talk. I cannot read. Otherwise my life would be very, very difficult."

"What happened to the boy next?"

This was a moment when Clarissa's visual imagery returned temporarily. "He was caught by the soldiers. They asked him to stop writing. He wouldn't. They killed him. He was only fifteen.

They burned away all his books. His soul felt very hurt and disappointed. He saw what the soldiers did to his work."

"What was his reaction?"

From this point onwards, she resumed her channeling mode.

"He made a vow that he would never publish any more. Never, ever ... it's worthless! There is lots of pain and sorrow. His soul is very confused. He was doing the right thing and not doing the right thing. He is so confused. Sharing is so wrong. Not sharing is not right. His soul is very tortured with these issues."

"So what happened to the boy afterwards?"

"He is right here ... on the couch here, talking to you."

I was startled, but decided to flow with the dialogue.

"Now that he has learned his lesson is he ready to change?"

"No."

"What is stopping him?"

"No (sobbing) ... Because no one will believe him. No ... he does not want to go through what he went through."

"What gives him the fear? It is a different life now?"

"I don't know what the difference is. They are not ready. I don't want this life to be the same, to be prosecuted like the other life. I was only fifteen. I did not even live to the fullest of my life."

The switching between the first person and third person was something that I distinctly noticed. I believed that was a sign that Clarissa wasn't prepared to relive and revivify the past life scene. The emotions involved were too painful.

"But now that you are in a different life, there are more opportunities to express yourself and there is no one to prosecute you."

"No. I do not want to shorten my life in this lifetime."

At this point, Clarissa while still in trance was able to sense that her catharsis was coming on, and she asked for a pillow. I was amazed, but quickly acceded to her request. Remaining in trance, she put the pillow directly in contact against her face and mouth and broke out crying. Then she screamed! She screamed aloud for two full minutes while allowing the sound to be muffled by the pressure of the pillow.

I had not expected her catharsis to be so intense. As a matter of fact, it was one of the most intense abreactions I had ever encountered in my practice.

There was a dramatic clinical improvement in Clarissa after she discharged her tension. The therapeutic result of abreaction is undeniable, and the theoretical basis is sound. The very process of becoming conscious over something that has hitherto been unconscious involves a discharge of emotional energy. The outcome is a relief of tension. The use of the cathartic method for therapy has been described as early as 1882. By encouraging patients to re-experience their problems and emotions under hypnosis, they may feel as if their accumulated emotions had become stuck on wrong lines and are now re-directed onto a normal path. Once discharged, there tends to be a fantastic feeling of relief that accompanies the dramatic disappearance of the symptom related to that experience. It is a feeling that inner healing has taken place.

"Take a deep breath ..." I said, as I noticed Clarissa's crying had significantly lessened.

I waited for another four minutes before her crying settled down to a soft, barely audible state.

"Continue to breathe slowly, and in a moment I will be bringing you to a place where you can obtain healing of your pain and unpleasant feelings ... When you are there, describe to me what you see ..."

"A waterfall ..." she began talking again. "And some flowers," she added, after a pause. I was delighted. Waterfalls and flowers often make good imagery for healing! I love working with whatever comes out of the patient's subconscious mind, because that helps me to obtain a better feel of the patient's inner reality. It is somewhat like a blind man groping in the dark and relying on other modes of perception to discern the nature of a world in which he is trying to attain some degree of control.

Given the extreme intensity of Clarissa's abreaction, I decided to put in additional effort to enrich the visual imagery.

"Concentrate on the beautiful flowers and the bright colors of the petals. Smell the sweet scent which they emit and which will bring you back to times of peace and happiness. Slowly walk past the garden of flowers and stroll towards the waterfall. As you get nearer, you hear the noise of the splashing water from the waterfall. It feels calm and soothing as the swashing sound of the waterfall cleanses you of your tension. You walk slowly towards the waterfall and at the count of three you step right into it ... one, you take a step forward ... two, you walk right into the waterfall, and three, you feel the water splashing down on top of your head, dripping down on your forehead, eyes, nose and face, coming down the sides of your neck, to the shoulders, dripping down the chest, arms, and waist and all the way down to your feet and toes ... draining away all the residual tension from your body. You continue to pay attention to the sound of my voice and as you do so you are reminded of your ability to speak and write.

"As you continue to heal yourself under the waterfall you will find yourself able to pronounce the words that come to you smoothly, naturally, and effortlessly. And each time ideas come to your mind you will know exactly what to say and what to write and you will take your time to prepare your thoughts before sharing them with your readers and your audience. Writing down your thoughts is satisfying, as is sharing them in public; these are gratifying actions bringing great joy and happiness. Remember, Clarissa, you are in total control of the words you speak and write at all times. Hearing you talk inspires other people. And writing down your thoughts equally amazes other people at the way your mind works. You have a vast amount of knowledge to share with others if you wish to do so, by writing down in a script or speaking in front of an audience. Speaking to a group of people allows you to share your knowledge with many people at the same time in both structured and informal manner. Formulating each thought in your mind in the correct sequence before uttering the words comes easily and naturally, as the waterfall continues to wash you of all your tension.

"Do exactly what you must do to deliver your message efficiently and clearly to your audience. Your excitement on the subject you are speaking on is motivating to other people. They understand the message you are communicating, the words you are using and speaking from now onwards. Each time you write down your ideas and prepare to stand in front of an audience you will do so with a lot of vitality and confidence. Hearing you speak inspires other people. Speaking to other people comes easily and naturally to you from now onwards. You know exactly what to write and say at the precise time.

"Finally you are getting control of your thoughts and actions in front of your audience and are now fully confident and self-assured. While you are under the waterfall, continue to go deep into the healing process. The water will cleanse you of all the agony and tension that has bogged you in your past life. Just take your time to visualize or imagine yourself preparing for a written assignment or speaking engagement ... that's right. You have done your homework on the subject you are going to speak on. You are relaying your thoughts to others in a confident and calm manner. Your breathing is paced and calm. You are focused, well rested and your facial expressions are in perfect harmony with your thoughts. You choose to deliver your message with a unique style. Each and every piece of writing and each and every speech you deliver will be a creation of your mind in its own right. Each and every time you prepare for your speaking engagement your enthusiasm will increase and you will feel yourself more and more confident of the words you choose to speak.

"Now, imagine yourself standing in front of an audience. Hear the applause of the audience as you step up to the front of the room. See the look of approval from the audience as they look at you and understand your message completely. Feel the pride within you as you are able to put your thoughts in writing with confidence and a self-assured manner to the audience. You know that it is your decision to be able to express yourself confidently to speak to a group and you accept this decision willingly and completely. And now you know you can and will do exactly what you must do to convey your message. You are now confident in formulating every thought in the correct sequence before saying the words. And this comes easily to you. You are confident in your ability to convey a message with integrity and enthusiasm and with style. And with each and every minute that passes as you stand before the audience it will give you more and more confidence in your ability to organize your thinking as you speak inspiringly in front of a group. Each performance will become easier and easier because you have a quick wit that knows exactly what to say at the exact moment."

It was a long healing script. After emerging her from trance, I passed her a box of tissue paper, following which I asked the nurse chaperone for a cup of warm water for her. During the subsequent dialogue, she commented on her own catharsis.

"The emotion was strong but fused internally. It is just the tension that I needed to let out through the screaming action. The screaming was the result of a lot of anger and frustration, because I cannot do what needs to be done."

Looking back, my therapy sessions with Clarissa had been increasingly more efficient in that she was taking a progressively shorter time to get to the root of her issue. I saw a lot of difference between what happened in this session as compared to what had happened when she first came to me for therapy seven months ago in April.

A fortnight later, Clarissa took up a new job as a life coach and trainer in a new company. She was specializing in the holistic development of children and youths with the goal of paving a foundation for their lifelong success. She was concentrating on the delivery of transformation programs that would unlock individual potential. It was then she began to realize the delivery skills she had and how much she enjoyed public speaking. No longer was there any fear.

Chapter Thirteen

Somaticized Pain

> "All our thoughts, regardless of their content, first enter our systems as energy. Those that carry emotional, mental, psychological or spiritual energy produce biological responses that are then stored in our cellular memory. In this way, our biographies are woven into our biological systems, gradually, slowly, every day."
>
> Caroline Myss, 1996

Three weeks later, Clarissa came back to me with yet another seemingly different problem. She had been experiencing a lower abdominal pain for the past nine months and the pain had recently intensified. It was a dull gnawing pain that was constant in nature and showed no specific pattern. She gave a severity of 7 on a visual analogue scale of 1 to 10. As she was someone with a high pain threshold, she had been putting the symptom off until recently when the pain had increasingly bothered her.

She consulted a gynecologist. After a thorough history taking and pelvic examination, the doctor could detect no gross clinical abnormality. He proceeded with transvaginal ultrasonography and the imaging again failed to show any pathology in her pelvic organs.

Yet, Clarissa was certain that her symptoms represented a significant malady. As I too could detect no physical abnormalities,

I arranged for her to undergo a CT scan of the abdomen and pelvis. The result of the imaging turned out to be completely normal when I checked the hospital's computer system three days later. Despite the absence of clinical abnormalities, I did not doubt that her pain was real.

In medical practice, such a situation would put the etiology of the problem into the category of *psychosomatic* illness. This term is often applied to imaginary illness created in the patient's head, with the implication that the symptoms are confabulated.

In truth, all physical and emotional issues are interconnected in life. *Psycho* means the mind and *somatic* refers to the body. The underlying meaning of the term *psychosomatic* is that the mind can make the body ill and the body can do likewise to the mind. In the practice of hypnotherapy, the therapeutic effectiveness of guided imagery lies in the latter's ability to approach from either the physical or the emotional side of the issue and heal both domains, often simultaneously.

Another term, *somaticization* is often used in psychiatry to describe a situation where unconscious anxiety has been converted into a physical symptom. This phenomenon is believed to be a defense mechanism against psychological stress. When an interpretation of the symptom breaks through into the patient's unconscious mind and the ego struggles to gain psychological insight, the core of the personality resists letting the content acquire a symbolic representation. It may be because the emerging insight is too much for the psyche to handle. The upsurge of the affect then releases itself into the body tissues as a physical symptom and forms a bulwark against integration.

From the regression therapist's perspective, the imprinting of past life traumas onto the body can be transmitted at a subtle emotional level as a physical symptom. When past life residues in the emotional body penetrate the etheric [22] body, emotional problems become embedded in the physical body as a clinical symptom.

On her own, Clarissa had adopted a spiritual approach. She sought the opinions of two psychic healers independently and obtained a consistent feedback. A blob of negative energy was noted to exist in her right lower abdomen and seemed to be related to a karmic debt.

It was on the afternoon of 14 December 2011 when she decided to ask me for another past life regression.

After some pondering, I decided to use the somaticized pain as a somatic bridge. By asking her to focus her mind on the lower abdominal pain and the associated feelings, she quickly entered into a past life.

"I see a dark spot in the middle of the pelvis," she began.

"Focus on that spot," I instructed. "See if there are any emotions that come up as you do so."

Suddenly, and without warning, Clarissa went into an abreaction. She grimaced, shook her head sideways in short, quick spurts and started to breathe heavily with the mouth open. This carried on for about two minutes. Grunting noises came from her throat. However, in addition, I heard chanting in the background. It appeared as if she was in agony.

"Tell me what's happening."

"It looks like some grieving process ..." she described hesitantly. In the meanwhile, I heard a soft crying voice in the background.

"Who is grieving?"

"An old woman. She lost her son."

---

[22] Etheric body is a term used in Theosophy to refer to the lowest layer in the human aura and is in immediate contact with the physical body. This is explained in detail in the Appendix.

The sound of wailing became louder in the background. I was intrigued.

"How did she lose her son?"

"It was a car accident ... The son was about twenty years of age. He was walking behind her. A white van drove up and struck him."

I heard the sorrowful wailing noise in the background distinctly while she was describing the scene.

"There is a lot of blood. She was there at the scene, crying. Her son's soul departed from his body ... The old lady kept crying at the body."

The sound of wailing evolved into a clear crying that was distinctly separate from Clarissa's voice.

"What happened next?"

"The son's soul is in heaven. He is calling for his mother, telling her not to be sad, and saying sorry that he has to go. His mum was scolding him for being unfilial and told him never again to come back as she will not forgive him."

There was a pause, and I waited.

"The son reincarnated ... I am the son. His mother came ... and that is the black spot!"

Wow! Awesome! Clarissa had identified the root cause of her pelvic pain in a very short time!

The "black spot" she described is often known as a *thought form* in the language of regression therapy. It is understood to be a projection of a person's consciousness onto another. It can be considered as the attachment of one energy form onto another, and the attachment exists in the form of an emotion, being sadness in this case.

"She's very angry and she wants revenge because he deserted her. The son explained that it was not his intention to desert her but she could not understand, no matter how he explained."

As a *thought form*, the black spot had no spark of divine consciousness at its center. Yet it seemed to have intelligence and purpose. It appeared to have a mind fragment of the mother who projected it. Using past life therapy in this instance allowed Clarissa to locate the actual incident when the *thought form* was conjured. Thereafter the emotions leading to the act could be resolved.

"There is a lot of pain, grief, and a lot of hope that the son will take care of her. She says wherever the son goes she will be there ... for his comfort. He left her and she's alone. From now on wherever he goes she will follow."

"Does the mother understand now?"

"No, no," came a very defiant voice.

"Talk to the mother."

"No," the same defiant voice responded. "She refuses to let anyone take away the son." Clarissa's voice came to the fore.

"Inject a spark of love into the mother's heart, and let her experience it," I intervened, and waited.

"How's the mother now? Is she ready to forgive?"

There was a pause. Something seemed to be at work. Emotions were building up, but Clarissa did not speak.

"Let me inject more love and forgiveness into her, and let it go into the mother's heart." Sobbing started and Clarissa went into an emotional turmoil.

"The mother has a strong sense of attachment," she said. "She is not willing to leave ... the sense of loss and belonging and the sense of attachment is too strong."

Given this situation, I decided that it was timely to bring in healing energy.

"In a moment, I am going to bring a healing light to the mother. At the count of three she will see a white healing light ... one, two, and three ... she now sees a ball of white light six inches in diameter, three feet above her. A ball of healing white light is slowly coming down and expanding in size ... it's about nine inches in diameter now and is coming nearer and nearer, gradually expanding to one foot in diameter, and getting brighter and brighter. It's getting much closer now and has increased to two feet in diameter. As it touches down it gets into the mother and she is sensing the healing power of the white light. Let her immerse in the light, stay with the experience of healing, of giving love and of letting go. And she knows that if she can let go she will no longer feel the pain and she will be able to forgive the son."

There was a pause. Healing seemed to be taking place.

"She wants to go *Home* ... the white light ... She wants to go to the white light."

"Good, in that case let the white light, which is all around her, bring her back all the way home, back to the Source where she can see her spirit guide and experience the power of love. Slowly imagine the white light enveloping around her, slowly lifting her up from the ground, and let her ascend bit by bit slowly all the way to the Source. Let her be there."

There were some noises in the background.

"She's giving me blessings ... She is throwing out some sparks of light."

"Very good. Has she come to terms with herself?"

"Yes," Clarissa said. (pause) "She says she is taking away all the shields or blockages from me. She asks you to give her some time."

There was a pause of one minute and I heard some heavy breathing.

"She's filling in the gap that she has taken before ... She's gone with the spirit guide now."

It was very clear by then Clarissa had become very comfortable with the concept of spirit guides. She understood them as entities from the *other side* and representing a mediator between worlds of being and non-being and of reality and nonreality. Such guides are around for our higher good, to help us to remember who we are, to let go of negative emotions and learn to love ourselves and others.

"Tell her to talk to the spirit guide and ask her if there is anything she wants to ask that she didn't have a chance to ask previously."

"She wants the spirit guide to give back her son. The spirit guide just smiles and remains silent. She smiles back and understands that the will of heaven cannot be changed. She has understood and she will abide that she has to go back to her own realm and leave the mundane world."

"Is she happy now?"

"The son reassures her that he knows what is happening and he is well protected. The Dark cannot touch him. She smiles, asks him if he is sure. The son smiles and reassures her that he is very safe, very well protected, even though the Dark is trying to reach him."

"Is the mother happy with the answer now?"

"She is hesitating. Her spirit guide assures her again. They have a conversation."

"What is the outcome of the conversation?"

"She is still worried about the son's safety. She is not really ready to let go. The spirit guide is explaining to her that she cannot protect the son if she continues to be in the son's body because that will create a problem for the son. It is not protecting, but she thought it was protecting. The spirit guide is explaining to her the mundane world and the human body works differently from spirit world. She has a wrong concept all this while."

"Does she understand now?"

There was a pause.

"This is new information for her and she is digesting it. She is asking what will happen to the lower part of the abdomen that is so painful. The spirit guide tells her those energies will resolve eventually if she does not continue to create havoc by existing in the body. The spirit guide tells her that he will work on those energies and she just has to let go because she is not helping. She is doing more harm than good. She asks a lot of questions and the spirit guide answers them. Then the spirit guide asks if she is ready to let go and she says 'yes' finally.

"She dissolves ... and she's gone. The spirit guide is here, doing what he promised her, sending energy to the body. He dissolves the negative energy and he is doing some healing ... says it is going to take a while."

"Stay with the experience."

"He tells me I have a very good mum. He says my body is going to have a different vibration. He overhauls every cell ... Healing is almost complete."

Forty-five minutes elapsed and the session came to an end. Clarissa was feeling good and vibrant after the session.

Later that same evening, Clarissa happily told me that her abdominal pain had vanished. She continued to remain completely pain-free in the days that followed.

It was the evening of 31 December 2011, two weeks after the therapy session, when Clarissa gave me a surprise call.

"Guess what! I am returning to Church!" she said excitingly.

"What happened?" I was utterly astonished.

"It's a long story ... but have a good start. Happy New Year and wish you many wonderful things ahead?"

"That is wonderful! Has anything triggered the change in you?" I pursued.

"Jesus, Mother Mary and my new guardian angel appeared to me a few days ago," she said. "I then decided to do my Penance after attending the Novena Church ... after some twenty to thirty years! I even brought my long-neglected altar stuff for the priest's blessings. In fact I just completed a Novena service today."

Fig. 17: *"I am on my way to the Church to receive Holy Communion."*

What bliss! I had not expected this to happen, but this is a happy ending after nine months of therapy. Of course, resumption in religious faith is only one outcome of successful therapy, and it is by no means the only way that change can manifest.

"You must be feeling great!" I commented.

"I have not attended a Novena since school days. I need to do it now to connect with Mother Mary again. I used to get all my petitions or requests come true whenever I asked her. In fact I am now on my way to the Church to receive Holy Communion to start afresh. It's amazing ... and I am making a comeback."

Making a *comeback* to one's faith is, in my experience, not necessarily the same as making a "return". Rather, it is more often a "re-turn", and indicates a new turning point in one's life where the individual finds new meaning.

"Congratulations! You are truly on a spiritual and transformational path," I said, holding back my amazement. "Can you tell me how did Jesus and Mary and your guardian angel appear?"

"I feel instantly connected to Mother Mary and I don't know why. I still remember the verses and the songs sung in Church even after not using them for so long. I confirm my connection is to Jesus through Mary, like the way it used to be during schooldays. Ha ha ... I am going to Church now. I can see and feel they are behind me."

"Really wonderful," I exclaimed. "Was it a sudden revelation and shower of grace?"

"It was a long journey to revelation for me," she admitted. "I actually had it all. I abandoned the faith due to ego and ignorance. The delivery of religious teaching during schooldays was not to my understanding. I have explored other faiths since. That was because their delivery was easier for me to relate. Now I find Catholicism has it all, after attending today's Mass. Now I am coming back to Jesus and Mother Mary, who has not given me up. What a spiritual journey! You have been such a gem friend and therapist who has journeyed with me. I am very grateful for your help."

"Wonderful, I feel blessed in being able to contribute to your spiritual journey."

Exuberance was growing. I felt rewarded. Clarissa had been unconsciously trapped in her expanded present for nearly three decades, so much so that time had not moved. Her psychological states and defenses had deterred her from making her wishes for happiness come true. With the response to therapy, she had progressively become more adaptive, successful, and symptom-free. She could now interact with the real world as a giving person. The time had come for her to release her immediate and long-term plans for her own future and return to Church. Although as a therapist I described her as "undergoing change", the truth is that she had found herself!

Section D

Scream in the Art Room

Chapter Fourteen

Snake Horror

"Valuable personal changes can occur, especially with highly charged negative images. On countless occasions, I have seen my clients meet octopi, mice, bats, giant spiders, imaginary monsters of all kinds and shapes, witches and sorcerers, and many other sinister beings. My clients were often frightened by them and felt they pictorially represented some deep-seated, unresolved aspects of themselves. Almost invariably I asked them to simply face those frightening creatures, become familiar with them, understand them, listen to their messages. The secret is always to have the courage to face the negative image and the patience to stay with it. Very often a transformation happens when we face it long enough and let the corresponding feelings freely emerge."

Piero Ferrucci, 1982

A phobia is an irrational fear that is out of proportion to the demands of the situation. The symptom is poorly understood, and as such often becomes a socially crippling disorder. While many adults may have some measure of insight into their phobia and recognize it as unreasonable, children and adolescents may not have the same awareness. They may not even know that their fear is excessive or unreasonable. All they may know is to avoid speaking about their fear to their schoolmates and avoid the specific object or situation at all costs.

It was a quiet weekday afternoon in the art room in Victoria Junior College. The air was still and a couple of students were concentrating on their painting and art assignments. A loud shriek suddenly filled the air. It came from one corner of the room as if someone was in horror. A group of art students rushed to the scene. Crouching in one corner was Lionel, seen in a cold sweat and tremors at the sight of a picture.

Someone had hand-drawn and painted a picture of a snake and left the drawing lying on one corner of the big table in the art room. It was a drawing of a coiled-up snake, with red stripes on its body and with the reptilian scales depicted in clear detail. Lionel stood there trembling in fear, and with rapid breathing. He grabbed the artwork, crumbled the paper vigorously with his hands and flung it onto the floor. The behavior looked strange and his fellow students were dumbfounded.

Lionel had always been a bright, intelligent and well-behaved model student in school. He had come from China on a scholarship to study in Singapore and had been excelling in all his subjects including Art. In fact his classmates had recognized his talents and nicknamed him a "perfect gentleman". This unruly behavior came as a total surprise to those who witnessed the incident.

Ten minutes later, Lionel's chest tightness diminished as he gradually calmed down. Someone brought him a glass of warm water and he quickly apologized for the commotion created. He explained that he had been experiencing an overwhelming fear of snakes since he was a child, and for as long as he could recall. He knew his behavior was irrational but simply couldn't help it. He had never dared to look at any images of snakes as a child. He was not aware of any environmental stressors that could have precipitated the extreme anxiety. As a rule he could not even tolerate any conversation that involved the mention of the word "snake".

What Lionel had was clearly a *phobia*. It is a form of neurotic anxiety where the anxiety response is very intense and focused on a specific object – in his case, the snake.

Many etiological factors have been attributed to the problem of childhood phobias. These include a genetic vulnerability to neuroticism and environmental stressors such as parental behavior and learning experiences that promote the acquisition of fear. Then there are psychologists who believe that phobia occurs in people because they have lost their sense of self-efficacy and are unable to respond to the situation presented to them. None of these factors seemed to be causative in Lionel's case.

Months later, Lionel finished his College examinations and was busy applying for University admission. At the same time he was preparing for a holiday break. Incidentally, Valerie, a classmate of his, remembered his unresolved problem and meekly drew his attention to the possibility of a remedy through hypnotherapy. His intrigue was immediately aroused.

Lionel found his way to my clinic at 11:00 am on 8 March 2012, and asked for advice for his condition. He had planned several holiday trips during this post-exam period and was hoping to find a remedy to his phobia before embarking on his University studies.

To my knowledge, several behavioral therapy approaches are available for treating phobias. The systematic desensitizing approach, for instance, is based on the theory that the maladaptive response is tied to the object through classical conditioning. Systematic desensitization would involve imagined exposure to the feared object, simultaneously accompanied by muscle relaxation.

Another approach is to use exposure treatments in vivo that are designed to generate a high level of fear response for the patient to experience continuously without escape, until the fear abates. It is based on the theory that prolonged exposure to the eliciting stimulus leads to extinction of the conditioned fear. This can be done either through *flooding* the patient with a highly intense stimulus, or through a *graduated exposure*. The addition of hypnosis to these behavioral techniques has long been known to enhance the results.

What is less well known, however, is that many causes of phobias are rooted in traumatic events of previous lifetimes. Hence a wide range of phobias can be successfully treated by past life therapy, particularly when the irrational fears are also strongly connected with the body and emotions. Intense recall and re-living of past life experiences often lead to remission of the symptom.

Lionel had no prior knowledge of hypnosis, and did not know what to expect. Upon hearing his story and the lack of obvious identifiable etiological factors, I suggested a past life regression. He was immediately intrigued and keen to find out more. After explaining to him what the therapy entailed, he excitedly agreed.

I spent the first twenty-five minutes with Lionel allowing him to go through a hypnotic relaxation. He was impressed with the level of relaxation achievable by hypnosis.

Phobias are always associated with a strong emotion and hence an affect bridge is an ideal approach for a seamless entry to a past life. The affect bridge works by emphasizing a common element between past and present lives. Fear is obviously the common element in this case. The technique then employs hypnosis to cross time lines from present to past.

"I want you to focus your fearful emotions at the sight of a snake until the emotion reaches a maximum ... Now use that emotion as a bridge to go back to a past life when you felt exactly the same way."

Lionel's entry into a past life scene was almost instant!

"I see a forest and a lake. I am alone. I am a boy in this past life, about twenty years of age. I see very tall trees ... it is daytime."

"What are you wearing?"

"A yellow shirt and black shoes made of cloth," Lionel said as he rapidly embodied himself into the scene.

Next the scene of the forest vanished and a new set of images flashed into his mind.

Lionel saw himself walking in the countryside in China. There were rice terraces and hills on both sides. As he walked further he saw village houses and soon he was stepping on a stone path. There were rocks on both sides. At a cliff on the far left was a Chinese pavilion[23].

Fig. 18: "The stairs where I encountered the snake." (Lionel's drawing)

"I see a street ... and some houses. I am walking on the street. I don't see any people around me. It's daytime ... I am now

---

[23] A Chinese pavilion is a covered structure without walls, meant to be a place for shade and rest

walking down a flight of stairs which leads from the end of the street."

"Where do the stairs lead to?"

"A beach."

"Where are you now?"

"I am near the bottom end of the stairs ... I see an image of a black snake with red dots forming a pattern on its skin. It is quite a big snake."

Fig. 19: Map of the snake location (Lionel's drawing)

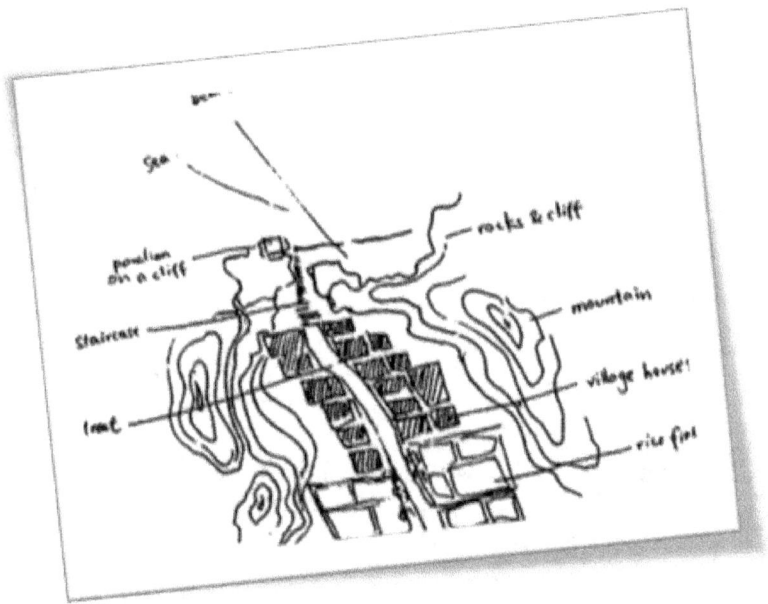

The story seemed to gather momentum.

"What is the diameter of the body of the snake?"

"The diameter is bigger than that of my arm, probably as big as that of my thigh."

"Where is the snake lying?"

"It's lying coiled up on the stairs."

"Look at the head of the snake and describe it to me," I instructed.

That instruction seemed to send shivers down Lionel's spine. His muscles were tightening up. His breathing turned shallow and rapid and he groaned a little.

"Red eyes," he said. It was a ghastly voice.

"What else?" I probed.

"White mouth."

"How far away are you from the snake?"

"Very near, about one to two meters away."

"Describe to me your emotions now."

"I am not afraid. I do not run away," he said.

I was surprised but allowed him to continue uninterrupted.

"I walk past the snake and go down the stairs," he said. "The snake turns its head."

"What happened when the snake turned its head?"

"Nothing," he hesitated.

"Look at the snake now and tell me how you feel."

'I am scared ... because it is opening its mouth."

"What did you do next?"

"I run away down the stairs. The snake follows. I am running to the beach. I suddenly see arrows being shot at the snake."

"Who shot the arrows?"

"Someone from a house near the top of the stairs. They look like some soldiers."

"What happened next, after the arrows were shot?"

"Looks like the snake died and they want to take it away ... Oh no ... I don't think the snake is dead. It is just not moving! Something invisible comes out of the snake. I don't know what it is."

There was fear in Lionel's voice.

"Use your feelings and find out what came out of the snake?"

"Some smoke comes out and it becomes the figure of an angel. It floats and goes up to the sky."

"Describe the angel figure to me."

"It's some kind of a Buddha or Buddhist figure. It looks mythical."

Mythical figures are often a way in which the *Higher Mind* speaks to the individual's consciousness. Their appearance under hypnosis often indicates a sufficient depth of trance.

"Describe your feelings to me."

"I am stunned. I ask myself: Am I going to be punished?" There was fear in his voice.

Suddenly Lionel was writhing about in agony. His body was swaying from side to side and twisted in a wavy motion. His breathing was heavy, and after about half a minute, he showed a few short gasps of breath. For a moment, I thought he was exhibiting an abreaction.

I waited for his writhing movements to slow down and instructed him to take a deep breath. He looked more relaxed after the breath, and I asked him what happened.

"I see black ..." he uttered while still remaining in trance. I was puzzled. I waited and decided to probe.

"Describe the nature of the blackness to me."

A minute of silence passed, and Lionel suddenly spoke.

"I feel I am inside the body of the snake," he mumbled.

For a while I was dumbfounded, but his earlier writhing movements and expression of agony suddenly made sense. I later learned from Lionel that although he did not visualize the actual swallowing action, he experienced a very strong and definite feeling of his whole body being inside the snake. It was very dark inside the cavity of the snake belly and the feeling was very real. He was aware that he was moving his body from side to side and he explained that he was passively following the wavy movements being inside the reptile's belly.

Silence followed, and it seemed like a life-changing moment. Following that Lionel said with an air of finale:

"That's the end ..."

As he ended the visualization experience, I felt it was too traumatic an experience for him to leave behind. Immediately I decided to put him through a healing experience.

"At the count of three I bring you to a place of healing ... describe to me what you see."

"I am inside a Buddhist temple. I see a wooden structure ... Some kind of Japanese-style temple."

Wonderful! I thought. A Buddhist temple makes excellent imagery for healing.

"Stay there and enjoy the spiritual environment of the temple. Listen to the sounds of the wind chime as the wind blows. Let the sound of the Buddhist prayers from the background calm you down. Imagine yourself sitting down meditating like everyone else. As you meditate you feel the peace coming back to yourself. You enjoy the silence, solitude and tranquility of the place. You love the sacred silence. That takes away all your fear. Your past has haunted you and the snake is a matter of the past and you are no longer scared of it. Remember that the snake is only a shadow in your mind. You are moving on. You meditate like a Zen Master. Feel the peace settling down into your inner self. Feel the love being showered on you. Feel the unconditional love you give to other people. Let go of all your anxieties. Let all the tension leave your body. Continue to be in this meditative position until the healing is complete."

Following his emergence from the trance state Lionel opened his eyes and heaved a sigh of relief. He was quite astonished at the thought of himself inside the snake body. Yet, this insight was central to his whole healing process.

It was 1:00 pm. I suggested to Lionel that he go for his lunch. In view of his travel plans, I asked him to return for a follow-up therapy session in the afternoon.

Chapter Fifteen

Art and Recovery

"I have explored the past lives of more than four thousand patients in my office and many thousands more in group workshops. I have witnessed incredible healing, as patients get rid of both emotional and physical symptoms after they recall the past life roots of their illness. Phobias and fears, grief, pain, and psychosomatic illness are all especially responsive to past life therapy."

Dr. Brian Weiss, MD, 1988

The deep-seated phobia seemed to have been released psychosomatically from Lionel after re-living the violent scenario. Excitedly, he called up Valerie during the lunch break to share his earth-shaking experience of the morning therapy. They had an unforgettable lunchtime together.

"Hey ... you know what! I was inside a snake!" he said, beaming with excitement. Valerie, who had been instrumental in getting him to seek treatment, was astounded! It was the first time she had heard him talking and joking about snakes ever since the day he scared everyone off in the school's Art Room! He now looked visibly relieved and relaxed.

Lionel returned to my clinic at 3:30 pm. Back on the couch, I induced him into a relaxed state and into the same past life quickly.

"Let yourself go back to the past event when you encounter the black snake."

"I see a bamboo forest ..."

"Tell me more."

"There is a path that leads into a house."

"Walk along the path and tell me what happens."

"There are monks. I see buckets of water ..."

Like in the morning session, the scene soon vanished and he gradually drifted into another scene.

"I am at the crossing of a street. It is a rainy day. The sky is quite dark. I see a house of Japanese style."

"Who is in the house?"

"A lady. She is a housewife. Doing housework. She offers me something. It's a bun."

"What happens next?"

"I see this Chinese-style mansion with a big garden."

"What is happening next?"

The scene was changing again.

"There is an image of a countryside. It is sort of a grass field, houses with white walls, gray roofs. I am walking into the Old Town."

"Tell me about the Old Town."

"It's very old, with narrow streets and high walls; I am on the street now."

"Walk along the street and tell me what happens."

"Long stairs. I am looking down the stairs."

"What did you see?"

"I see clouds floating in the air. I am on the stairs. There is a snake on the middle of the stairs. It is the same snake that I saw earlier ... black in color ... very big red dots on the skin."

"Look at the eyes closely and describe them."

In using guided imagery, images are perceived as direct manifestations of a patient's emotions. In other words, they are not deceptive but indicate the patient's true self. Hence, efforts in attending to these internal images often help with the patient's inner expression and, therefore, healing.

"Distended eyes ... look red," Lionel said calmly, without the fearful emotion he had displayed in the morning session.

"What happens next?"

"I am touching the snake. It feels like a small pet."

I was both surprised and amused. He gave me the sense he had been partially desensitized of his irrational fear after the morning therapy.

Soon, the snake moved away from the stairs to the beach.

"What are your emotions at this stage?"

"Mixed emotions. I don't know why I am touching it, although I still feel scared."

"What did the snake do when you touched it?"

"The eyes are looking down on the ground. The snake body forms a circle. I take the snake up and carry it with me. Don't know why I do it ..."

I felt increasingly reassured that a major part of Lionel's phobia had vanished.

"The snake is in the basket now. I walk away. The snake comes out of the basket. It moves towards me. It is at my feet and climbing onto my right back. I think it is going to bite me."

"Did it bite you?"

"I don't think so ... because I do not feel the pain.

"It moves upwards towards my upper body. It is on my right arm now."

"What happens next?"

"I think the snake has bitten me," he said calmly without any evidence of panic.

"I feel the pain in my right arm. The right arm has become numb. It feels warm one moment and cold at another moment ... it is not very painful. The snake leaves me and goes to the field."

"What happens next?"

"I see the mountain behind the field. It is a beautiful scene." Lionel remains very calm.

"What happens to the snake?"

"I can't see it now."

"How does your arm feel now?"

"It is not painful, just numb. It doesn't bleed. The skin color of the arm has become purplish."

"What happens next?"

"I recover quite fast. I get onto a motorcycle and go away."

"Where did you go to?"

"To another town. I see people selling stuff ... There is a lake. It is a beach by the sea. It is the same beach where I saw the big snake during the last session. There are no more snakes now. I stand by the sea and I feel happy."

I emerged Lionel from hypnosis after this with a countdown of five to one.

Comparatively this afternoon session was far more relaxing compared to the morning therapy.

Over the next two weeks, Lionel enjoyed a wonderful holiday in Thailand and Cambodia. He returned to my clinic on the afternoon of 23 March 2012, still very keen for a third session. He was due to return home to China soon. He had brought along his drawing that showed the village street and the stairs where he encountered the past life snake.

Being an art student Lionel had good skills in drawing and painting. I was delighted. Communication through art production is really another form of therapy. While the medical community has yet to openly embrace the power of Art Therapy, artists are increasingly aware that images play an essential role in the processing of past experiences. Artistic drawings by the patient can provide meaningful therapeutic interaction without the need for verbal communication.

By then, Lionel was relatively free from phobia but I wanted to reinforce the desensitization. Once again he was quickly regressed back to the same past life.

"I see a boat in a lake and a person is in the boat. It's a small wooden boat ... I am also on the boat. I am feeling motion sickness. The wind is quite strong and is blowing the boat in the direction of the beach."

I noticed that Lionel's body began to wriggle from side to side.

"What happened?" I asked.

"I am drifting with the boat. The boat is not going towards the beach. It is going towards the rocks instead," he said while his breathing was turning heavy.

"What happened next?"

"I am now out of the boat and am standing on a rock. There is a cave. I am at the entrance. Oh ... I see the snake ... It is the same snake that I saw previously. It's on the cliff, outside the cave, above the entrance."

"What happened next?"

"The snake moves away. I look into the cave. It is a limestone cave." The breathing turned heavy again.

"It's a very big entrance. I walk in. I am playing inside the cave. I see the same snake with red dots. It's quite big. The diameter is that of my thigh ... the snake slips into a pond in the cave."

"What are your emotions?"

"I do not feel scared ..." Lionel said calmly.

"I see a snake in the center of the pond, coiled up. It is a white snake. I was thinking this white snake and the black snake may be a pair."

Suddenly Lionel's lips were twitching on the right.

"The snake jumps out of the water." Lionel's right hand was moving involuntarily with a snake-like motion and his right foot was swaying from side to side.

"I am running out of the cave. The snake is behind me."

Fig. 20: "It is a big black snake with red dots." (Lionel's drawing)

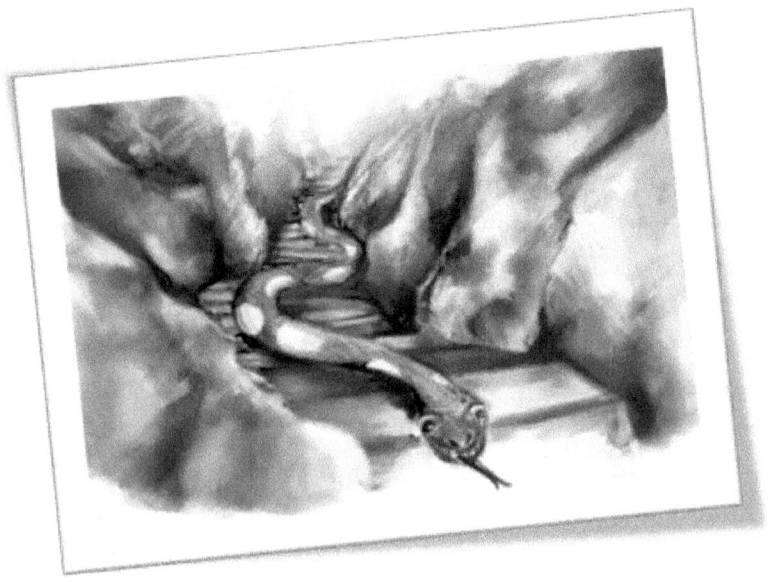

"What are your emotions?"

"Fear. I am panicking ... I am at the edge of the road. I see smoke a few meters away. Behind me is the sea. I stop. I see smoke in front of me. I jump back into my boat. I am rowing my boat ... the snake also jumps into my boat. We are at either ends of the boat. I am rowing towards the beach ..."

"Go to the point where you reach the beach."

"So tired," Lionel said with a sigh. "I reach the beach. I get down from the boat. The snake is still at the other end of the boat, coiled up. I push the boat with the snake inside to the sea. I am sitting down on the beach, very tired. The boat has drifted away," Lionel sighed with relief.

The session ended on a high note. Lionel had confidently got over his phobia, and I confirmed it by testing him with several colored pictures of snakes retrieved from the Internet. He smiled and talked calmly about them, describing how he used to panic in the past.

Lionel returned home to China the following week, feeling relieved and relaxed. He went on his holidays in South Eastern China where he toured the cities of Nanjing, Suzhou, Xitang and Hangzhou. He informed me that he had been offered a place at University College of London to pursue his Architectural studies and was looking forward to it. He felt extremely happy that he had ridden himself of his phobia and wanted to move on in life.

On 10 May 2012 he drew a picture of the snake that he had visualized under trance, crawling along the staircase of the rocky slope that was leading to the beach. The big bulging eyes, the white teeth and fangs, the bifid tongue and the elliptical patches or "dots" as Lionel described, were all clearly illustrated in his drawing.

I received the picture from him through email.

"This is the best evidence to show that you have recovered from your phobia!" I told him.

Appendix

Healing & Past Life Therapy

Introduction

Medicine is traditionally considered a *healing* profession, but its practical focus has always been centered on the perspective of *curing*. A *cure* is understood to be the end or riddance of a disease condition associated with physiological restoration brought about by a medication or a procedure. For incurable diseases, the aim is for a *remission*, or a temporary end to the signs and symptoms caused by the disease. In complex diseases such as cancer where the concept of *cure* is assessed by comparing disease-free survivals of patients against matched controls, an indefinite remission is considered as good as a cure.

The concept of *healing*, on the other hand, is a broader one going beyond the physiological restoration of diseased states as indicated by physical signs and symptoms.

Hermeneutics of Healing

Medicine's interpretation of *healing* has been constructed from the physiological processes centered on the restoration of biological function. However, in the holistic paradigm *healing* is about attaining wholeness for the individual, and is an intense personal experience. The *healing* process involves the individual's reconciliation of the meaning ascribed to the disease or distressing events in his life with the perception of his personal wholeness. In other words, it is a personal experience of the transcendence of suffering.

Medical epistemology has its roots in Cartesian thinking[24], and teaches that nature is divided into two independent realms, one for the mind and another for the body. As a result Medicine is often practiced with the assumption that nature works according to physical laws and clinical phenomena are explained in mechanistic terms. Sometimes the diseased human is conceptualized as being confined in a physical body requiring technological intervention. By likening the workings of the human body to a machine constructed from several parts, sickness tends to be understood in terms of deranged function of individual body parts. This worldview unfortunately predisposes the practitioner to lose sight of the patient as a *holistic* being.

The term *holism* implies that the patient is viewed in his totality rather than from the angle of a specific set of symptoms. This perspective is derived from a model of the interrelationship between the physical, mental, emotional and spiritual dimensions of the patient. All humans are viewed as interacting dynamically with his or her environment. Each person is seen as a unified system or a coordinated whole, rather than as a container for a body, a mind, emotions and a soul. Process and interrelationships are emphasized, more than the discrete parts and causal relationships. At the same time, importance is placed on the interconnectedness between individuals and all of nature.

The *holistic* view emphasizes the value of a unique individual in a specific point in time. Hence two people with the same set of symptoms may be treated very differently. The view is that our wellbeing is in our hands and the effectiveness of treatment rests largely with our motivation and confidence to initiate the healing from within ourselves. At the same time, the focus on individual uniqueness leads to an emphasis on flux and transition rather than

---

[24] René Descartes (1596-1650) was a French philosopher and mathematician, credited as the father of analytic geometry and the first thinker to emphasize the use of reason to develop the natural sciences.

on static conditions. The reader may have noted that the theme of "moving on" has been central to the case studies in this book. Life transitions are characterized by further growth, and continuous learning is much valued as the means to attain the individual's unique potential. Integral to the holistic paradigm are two features: (a) the linkage between stress and susceptibility to disease, and (b) the relation of spiritual wellbeing to health and sickness. Furthermore, primacy is placed on the aspects of mind, belief systems, attitudes and emotions of the individual in determining disease onset and severity as well as the course of treatment.

In holistic care, health-promoting lifestyle patterns are heavily emphasized. Health is defined in terms of integration and harmony while illness is viewed as an opportunity for positive growth. More importantly, healthcare is primarily a matter of the responsibility of the individual rather than the provider. The therapist functions as a facilitator of healing by mobilizing innate healing capacities residing in the patient. There is an egalitarian relationship between the therapist and the patient. The patient is not viewed as a target for which a biological intervention is given. In fact holistic healing involves two active systems that are interacting with each other and ultimately both are changed. It is perceived as a co-creative process in which the patient simultaneously heals and teaches the healer.

What is Regression Therapy?

Regression therapy is one example of a holistic therapy. It helps the patient to relive forgotten or repressed experiences that contain unhealed emotional wounds which may be triggering unexplained symptoms. At its core, it is an advanced healing technique that leverages on the hypnotic state. Memories buried deep in the mind are brought out. Unlocking those emotions under trance brings insights into how present complaints have their origin in those repressed and ignored experiences. Taking patients back through their subconscious mind to the time before their present is known as past life regression.

The purpose of facilitating patients to recall their past lives is to draw on their innate healing power. The focus is not on offering explanations of past life phenomena nor promoting the doctrine of reincarnation. The believer of reincarnation would view the soul dwelling within the body at birth as having lived many lifetimes in many other bodies before. As a result of accumulated merit or worthlessness of previous actions, the karmic consequences manifest as a symptom in the current life. The Jungian analyst on the other hand would view the past life phenomenon through the concept of the *collective unconscious*, into which the individual is deemed to have the capacity to dip into the vast collective memory of mankind. Whichever perspective we take is unimportant. It is the ultimate analytic insights emanating from the inner psyche during the regression process that is instrumental to healing.

Knowledge of how one's past life actions relate to one's current life problem enables a reorganization of the understanding of the issue at both the cognitive and the emotional level. The resulting change pervades the patient's entire being and results in alterations in his outlook and lifestyle. Dynamic factors that have hitherto maintained the symptoms lose their influence and the end result is that of a transformation. Whatever has been disharmonious in the past is now rebalanced and a new equilibrium is established. The renewal restores the patient to wholeness and peacefulness via new beginnings. The patient is now able to make a fresh start because his hopes, dreams, and aspirations are revived.

The Nature of Past Lives

Past lives are a cumulative set of lessons that we have learned from the former incarnations of the soul or the higher self.

Sometimes, the fears or emotions from previous lives may be carried over and impact on our existence in the present life.

Retrieving an individual's past life content as a form of psychotherapy is of relatively recent development. Attempts to explain the notion of past lives is tricky. In my training, I have been taught to work with past lives on the premise that the soul of an individual is *reborn* into a new body for the purpose of understanding and resolving negative emotions incurred in previous lifetimes. Experiences or feelings in a current lifetime can be traced to an experience in a past incarnation. However, a belief in reincarnation is not necessary for past life regression to work, nor a prerequisite to benefit from past life therapy.

In explaining the concept of past life therapy, Woolger used the analogy of old, corrupted program files that interfere with the running of a computer program. Problems at the psychic level such as depression, phobias and compulsive disorders are like corrupted files. They came from emotional patterns embedded deep in our past lives. Past life therapy is like fixing these corrupted files to allow the program to function properly again.

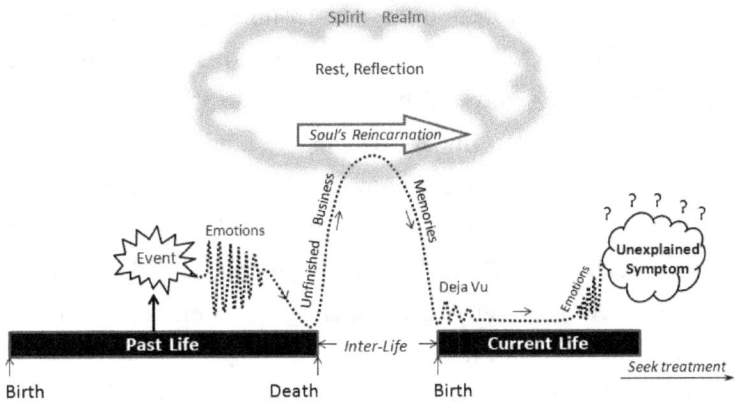

Fig. 21: "Pathophysiology" of a Past Life Issue

Many patients carry with them puzzling patterns of guilt, limiting thoughts and irrational fear in their lives. The psychiatric practitioner, unable to pinpoint the origin of these issues, may tend to label such problems as a general anxiety disorder. Yet from the viewpoint of past life therapy, such symptoms are not surprising because we recognize that they may have originated from the experience of another lifetime. When we look for the trauma or event that has caused the psychological disturbance in the wrong place, the treatment just doesn't work.

Milton's past life dream in Section B is a good illustration of the physical impact of past life emotions. He experienced a sudden and incapacitating backache one morning when he woke up in the military camp. He couldn't account for the strange symptom occurrence, but deep down he knew it originated from his inner psyche. He dreamt and the military environment connected his psyche with one of his past lives during which he was at war.

In that life he was a Crusader fighting the Muslim Turks. He was captured by the Muslim soldiers and that "event" became a turning point in his past life. The trauma he experienced during the subsequent torture by his captors created turbulent emotions that stayed with his soul. He was wounded by a spear in the back. The pain sustained from the stab wound generated strong emotional residues. These were carried over to his present lifetime and manifested in his physical body as an unexplained backache. The torture culminated in his death. He was stabbed by the Turkish captors in his chest with a spear. The heightened consciousness of the violent death imprinted the dying thoughts and feelings on his soul. Powerful karma was created. Milton's pain and fear were brought over to the present life as a birthmark on his chest at the entry point of the spear.

The soul's anguish of unfinished business as a Crusader fighting in a Holy War survived that lifetime to give Milton a sense of unexplained affinity with major world religions in his current life. He had a strong passion for spiritual literature and an urge to continually search for meaning in life. Uncovering the past life through the dream allowed his inner body tension to be released and his backache and back muscle spasm to vanish, once he understood the origin of his symptoms.

Fig. 22: The "Anatomy" of Inner Healing

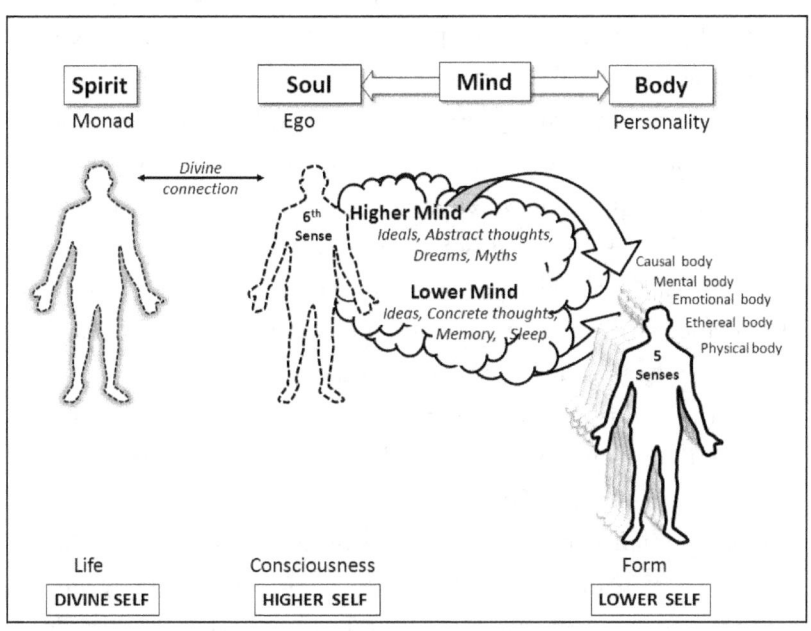

But, what exactly is our understanding of the *soul* vis-à-vis the *mind* and the *body*? How does the *soul* survive the death of the body? What makes it an unchanging entity that traverses lifetimes?

Body, Mind, Soul and Spirit

The *body* refers to everything that is described under the structure and function of the human being and whatever pathological change that occurs during illness. The *mind* refers to the psychological reactions to our maladies and what we feel about being sick. The *soul* is viewed as the spark of life within us. It inhabits our physical body, manifests as our ego and contributes to the continuity of human consciousness. What we understand as *consciousness* is intimately linked to the physiological state of the body and connected through the vehicle of the *mind*.

There is consciousness that exists throughout the whole of the Universe that brings life to us all. Part of the consciousness is split off and is given an opportunity to experience and grow in human life. This part that is split off is what we call the *soul*. Even after clinical death, this part of the consciousness survives death.

The way the *soul* grows is to experience difficult situations and to master aspects of emotions. It is as if the Earth is a classroom for the soul which goes through its life lessons one by one until it masters the lesson and then proceeds on to the next one. The *soul* is perceived as being immortal and endowed with all the divine attributes of its Creator. It has free will and makes its decision to be born in certain times and places.

The *soul* is unbound by time and space. It is the seat of the *Higher Self* or a wise inner advisor that patients may sometimes call upon during therapy. The purpose of our *Higher Self* is to provide wisdom, guidance, compassion and love to assist us in manifesting our true reason why we are on Earth or our karmic purpose. At a more mundane level, calling upon the *Higher Self* helps problem solving.

The *soul* is buried deep inside our psyche and it speaks to us through dreams where it often takes the form of archetypal symbols, motifs and myths. As the case studies in this book show, the archetypal symbol can take many forms, including a noble animal, a wise mentor or a religious figure. These images convey advice and messages which resonate with our deeper need for guidance and transcendence.

The *soul* is also what makes the individual unique. It is how the individual relates to others and how he understands himself. In contrast the *spirit* is how the individual relates to the Divine. The *spiritual* aspect of illness refers to what goes on in the deeper levels of the psyche and to the special meaning the individual attaches to the illness in the course of his life.

In the context of this book, the meaning of *spirituality* is sharply differentiated from that of *religion*. Religion refers to a belief system of a particular group of people whereas spirituality refers to the realm of the human spirit, or that part of humanity that is not related to the bodily experience.

There is a transcendental spiritual quality within every individual and is a potential that is often sought after. This is sometimes called a *spark of the divine*. When the spiritual forces inside a person can no longer be held in check, as in a calling, the sudden surge of energy gives rise to a burst of vision. Once awakened, this spiritual quality helps the individual to gain a sense of balance, peace and harmony with his sorrows and confusions of life. The healing that develops thereafter gives the individual a heightened state of mental illumination and aliveness. Something is changed. He finds new meaning and he will not be the same again. It is the awakening of this spiritual part of the individual that clarifies his meaning and purpose of life. It dispels his doubts and offers solutions to many of his problems.

A basic energy source exists and allows the *soul* and *mind* to interact with the biological tissues of the *body* to produce a conscious living being. In the material world all elements can be traced back to an origin and a constant cycle. It is a cycle in which matter evolves, disintegrates and returns into being. Our consciousness is subject to similar changes. When tracing our present consciousness backwards during regression, we are following the continuity of the *soul* and *mind* into an infinite dimension where there isn't a beginning, very much like the origin of the universe. Hence, there must be successive rebirths for the continuity of the *soul* and *mind* to exist.

Behavioral patterns are part of *energy fields*. According to principles of Physics, energy fields do not vanish, and can only be transmuted. Hence, energy fields generated in previous lifetimes can be brought forward into the current life as repeated vibrational patterns in the form of sub-personalities. Such experiences are stored in a mental repository which continues from one lifetime to another. In other words, it is our decision to choose our parents, friends, lovers and enemies. We cannot blame other people for our bad childhood, a difficult marriage or for our present problems. Intriguingly, the content from this mental depository can be recovered while the patient is in an altered state of consciousness during hypnosis.

The types of unfinished business that emerge during a past life regression may be better understood within the framework of subtle energy fields in the body, as explained in traditional yoga teachings:

(i) the *causal (spiritual) body* – is the highest subtle level that veils the soul and is the vehicle of the Higher Mind. It relates to what Jung considers as the *collective consciousness*. It is through this field that Gerald found his psychic connections to the spirit of Mei Fung, who he was so strongly involved with in his past life (Section A).

(ii) the *mental body* – is the locus of the individual's conscious and unconscious thoughts and can influence his life patterns and self-image. This is the energy field through which Gerald carried his obsessive thoughts: e.g. "I got you and your mum into trouble" and "Had I not run upstairs you would not have been caught."

(iii) the *emotional (astral) body* – is the locus of the feeling residues from past events and strongly affected by negative thoughts from the mental body. For example, Gerald's unresolved anger about his betrayal and his feeling of hopelessness in his warfare against the Japanese soldiers were carried in this field.

(iv) the *ethereal (etheric) body* – is where the repressed feelings from the emotional body will lodge to produce organic symptoms. This energy field is quite close to the physical body. Gerald's vivid memories of his head being dunked under water and the unhealed emotional trauma was carried in this field and caused a physical dysfunction – water phobia in his current life.

The term *Inner Self* is used repeatedly in various parts of this book. It refers to the concept of self-realization. It also describes the profound spiritual awakening where the illusory self-identity image awakens to the individual's true, divine, and perfect condition. The case studies in this book illustrate clearly how the patient's ability to connect with the *Inner Self* accelerates the healing process.

In the clinical setting, it is not uncommon to encounter past life issues presenting as unexplainable symptoms or irrational emotions. Typically, such patients would have already sought medical attention extensively, only to be told that nothing is organically wrong with them. Some may be advised to accept and live with the discomfort while others are prescribed psychotropic drugs on the premise that the chemical imbalance existing in their brain synapses has caused their symptom.

The therapeutic principle by which past life regression is used to deal with such symptoms is by revealing the unconscious content of the psyche to the conscious mind in order to alleviate psychic tension in the patient. In doing so, it helps the individual to act with more conscious awareness than unconscious reactions permit. In this regard, it is very similar to psychodynamic or psychoanalytical psychotherapy. There is however one major difference. The *psychoanalyst* for the most part listens passively to the patient in the conscious state and offers insightful interpretations. In contrast, the *regression therapist* actively dialogues with the patient under trance, and directs and helps him to rework the stories, images and ideas coming from his unconscious realm. Flashes of insight commonly emerge as a result of this kind of interaction and are fundamental to the healing process.

Neurophysiology of Hypnosis

In hypnosis, the patient is asked to close the eyes to blot out visual stimulation, so that there is strong concentration on the therapist's verbalizations. It is like music lovers in a concert who, wanting to concentrate on the auditory experience, recline their heads backwards and close their eyes to listen better. As the individual detaches from the external world and devotes his full attention to therapeutic ideas and suggestions, he often experiences profound perceptual and affective changes.

Hypnosis is often used to bring a person into a past life. With the deep relaxation made possible through hypnosis it becomes easier for one to tune into memories of another part of one's consciousness. It is like tuning the old-fashioned radio where one initially hears a hiss, but as one continues to tune and get into the resonance frequency of a station, one can hear the sound of the radio quite clearly.

The patient under hypnosis has recognizable patterns of electrical brain activity. The brain normally generates voltage fluctuations resulting from ionic current flows within the nerve cells. This spontaneous electrical activity of the brain can be recorded by placing electrodes on the surface of the scalp.

Fig. 23: EEG Waveforms in Various Mental States

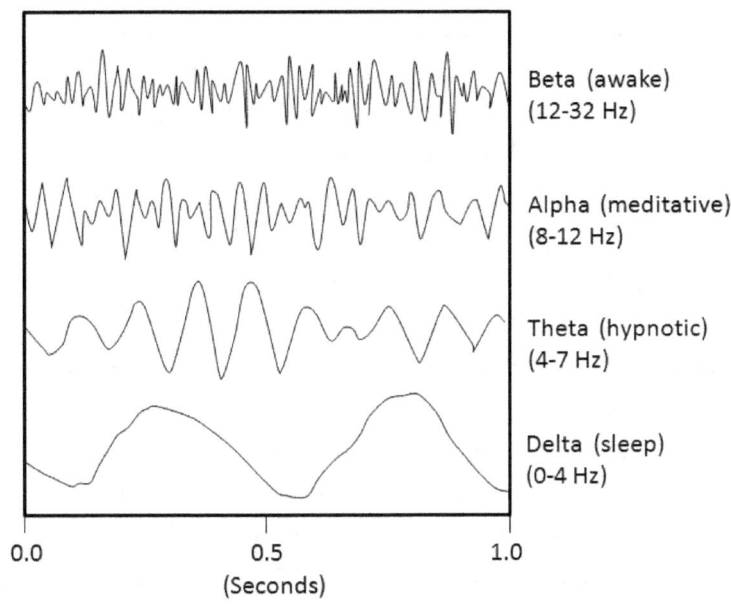

In the normal awake state, the voltage measurements appear as a waveform of the frequency of 12 to 32 Hz on the electroencephalogram (EEG). We call these *beta* waves. Low amplitude beta waves with varying frequencies are a feature of active, busy thinking and active concentration. As the individual begins to calm down, closes his eyes, mentally relaxes himself and enters into a meditative mode, those neural oscillations of 8 to 12 Hz in frequency will emerge. We call these *alpha waves*. These alpha waves represent the activity of the visual cortex in the occipital part of the brain in the idle state and are the dominant waveform observed in people performing meditation.

Mindfulness is a related concept. It is being used in modern psychology to describe this state in which a person is calm, non-judgmental and aware of the present state of his bodily functions. This term is derived from the concept of Buddhist meditation where *mindfulness* is considered an important faculty in the path of enlightenment.

As the patient's relaxation continues to deepen with one-pointed concentration under the direction of the therapist, even slower electrical brain waves may emerge. These are in the range of 4 to 7 Hz and are called *theta* waves. This is a state of mind which is often associated with day-dreaming, mental creativity and the development of spiritual connection. We call this the *hypnotic state*. It is important to emphasize that it is not a state of sleep, which is associated by the much slower *delta* waves (0 to 4 Hz). Both hypnosis and sleep are altered states of awareness and one may merge into the other.

Deep hypnotic states are usually characterized by strong *theta* states. However, most past life memories are retrievable with the patient in the lighter *alpha–theta* state. One thing to bear in mind is that it is possible for an individual to be in one or several levels of brain states simultaneously because a mix of different wave types are present at any one time. In fact, the processing of past life memories during regression relies on the ability of the patient to retain sufficiently strong *beta* waves while he sinks into deeper states of relaxation.

Hypnotizability

The power to hypnotize rests not with the therapist but with the patient himself. The ability of the patient to enter a hypnotic state is dependent heavily on his beliefs and willingness. It is important to bear in mind those patients who under the influence of alcohol and addictive drugs may not be hypnotizable. Generally hypnotizability tends to be influenced by the following factors:
(i)   Ability to comprehend directions given by the therapist.
(ii) Ability to regulate imagined situations – Imagery is an important aspect of imagination and guided imagery is almost

always used as a technique in hypnosis. The ability to accept different realities in trance plays an important role in hypnotizability. The individual who is fantasy-prone or inclined towards day-dreaming is often easily hypnotizable.

(iii) Willingness to rely on the therapist for control of the situation - Subjects who are non-analytic in their thinking tend to be hypnotized more readily. This is partly because they are more ready to accept new things without questioning the reason and partly because over-analytic minds tend to be less imaginative. The mind has to truly believe in an alternate reality at the suggestion of the therapist. The patient's trust in the therapist and his rapport with him are crucial determinants. Suspicion usually negates hypnotizability.

(iv) Motivation of the patient - A pre-founded interest in understanding the mind, a positive attitude towards hypnosis and a motivation to see positive effects all help towards better hypnotizability.

Regression Technique

In hypnosis, the therapist taps into the power of the patient's unconscious mind. The conscious mind possesses an unreliable memory. On the contrary, the unconscious mind has a marvelous memory which registers the minor events and the less important acts of our existence without our knowing it. Furthermore it accepts with unreasoning docility what is being told and suggested without question.

(a)   Induction

Bringing a patient into an altered state of consciousness is done largely with a combination of mental relaxation, verbal suggestion and sensory imagery. The counting of a patient down a staircase is a simple way of deepening the hypnotic state.

Upon deepening the hypnotic state, the entry into a past life can be achieved by one of several techniques. Visualization and guiding of the patient along a passageway and through a door that "opens" into a past life is a simple method of providing a direct entry. Alternatively the taking of the patient down an imagined elevator to the level where the significant lifetime lies provides an entry that can be easily embellished by the imagination. Likewise the boarding of a train that goes back in time to the destination of the previous lifetime can be equally effective.

Fig. 24: Past Life Therapy

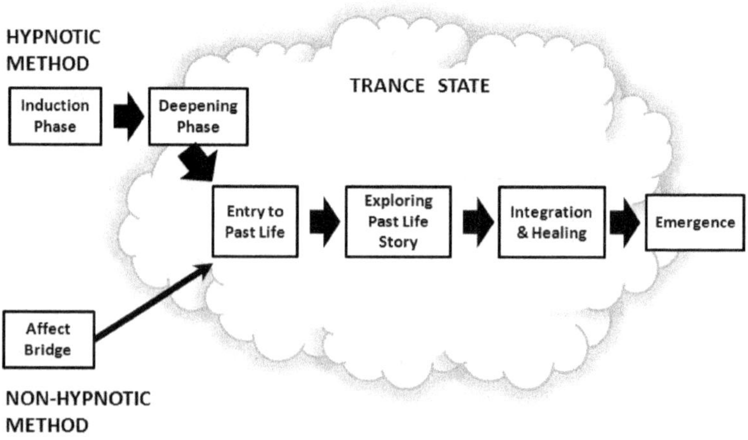

At this stage, some patients go straight into a past life and the past life story becomes clear from the word go. For some others they need to be eased into it more gently. The therapist may need to ask the patients what they can see, hear or feel; who they are in that past life and what they are doing at that moment. Sometimes the patient may focus on only one particular event and at other times he may get into multiple significant events in that lifetime.

Some other patients may jump from one lifetime to another in the same session.

(b)   Affect Bridge

Hypnotic inductions are not always necessary for past life entry. The use of the *affect bridge* is a quick and convenient alternative. It is a technique of following a feeling, body sensation or an emotion associated with the patient's core issue backwards into a past life. The therapist chooses a particular emotion on the basis of the patient's symptomatology at the start of the session. Examples of how the emotion is chosen and bridge identified abound in this book. Common emotions encountered in patients coming for therapy include anger, sadness, guilt, fear, helplessness, etc. The therapist then gives suggestions to amplify the intensity of the emotion and the evoked affect is used as a *bridge* or link to the past. The patient is told to go back to a time in a past life (or an earlier time in his present life) when he felt the emotion in exactly the same way.

An intense intra-psychic focus is achieved by concentrating on a combination of the mental, emotional and somatic components of the bridge. The one-pointed nature of the affect precipitates the patient into a previous lifetime without the need for any hypnotic induction. The patient's unconscious mind would automatically select an event from a previous life that reflects the emotions of his current life concern.

Subsequent to entry, the retrieval and processing of past life memories follow a consistent pattern. In the first stage, the patient relegates the control of his own conscious process and identifies himself with the figure of an imaged person on a dream-like journey. This journey often involves a replay of significant past life issues and trauma. The therapist relegates his role as co-explorer of the patient's past life. The purpose is to help the patient to relive the emotions in the body of the person as though the patient is the past life person himself.

Using simple, open-ended questions the therapist helps the patient move within the time frame of the past life being examined. The changing conditions and phases of that lifetime now become the patient's vicissitudes. He relives his past life experience like watching a replay of a video-recording of a former lifetime of himself.

The Regression Experience

During a past life regression, the recalled memories are experienced by different patients in different ways:
(a) like viewing a movie,
(b) in the form of hazy visual impressions or images that rapidly appear or disappear,
(c) as quick auditory impressions,
(d) as information conveyed through thought, or
(e) as an intuitive experience that allows the individual to instantly "know" what is happening.

The images and scenes are sometimes associated with a sense of familiarity. The patient may recognize people and places from his present life and the past life story helps to clarify current relationships.

Patients who have been taken from present to past life experience often report feeling as if they have left the body and are watching the "movie" from another plane. Most patients find that the emotions evoked by a past life regression are very powerful, generally more so than those evoked by a movie or a novel. Often these emotions are described as "overwhelming" or "incredible" and may be accompanied by tears and crying. For that reason, many feel that the experience is likely to be "real".

Exploring the Past Life

As the regression proceeds, the therapist invariably uses open-ended and non-leading questions to guide the patient to sense and describe his surroundings. The hypnotic trance in a past life regression is relatively light and the patient is entirely aware of everything and will remember everything. As he listens to the therapist, he responds by continuously talking to share what he is experiencing. It is also because of this light level of trance that many patients find the regression experience fascinating. Images seem to be forming from haziness and transit into other images or scenes with the prompting of the therapist. Some may describe the experience as a "forced dream" or "a mind grasping for answers." Many others often ask: "Is this real or imagined? Did I make it up?" or "Is my mind playing tricks on me?" Yet, the moment they experience the vivid imagery, the depth of what they have visualized and the intensity of the emotions evoked, they begin to wonder where the images could have come from. Soon they lose the sense that they have involuntarily made it up.

The therapist may use a past life regression to explore a patient's current life events and his relationship to those he knows in his current life, and see how they were connected in a past life. This may help to bring clarity to those issues, such as a lack of personal power, unexplained anxiety, career dissatisfaction, etc., that seem to be blocking the patient from progressing in his current life. Commonly the patient may find meaning in his explained illnesses.

Not all patients will be able to enter a past life. This is especially so if they have been inadequately prepared for the session. Some have misconceptions about hypnosis or their conscious minds are too strong to relinquish control. They may be afraid of "getting stuck" in hypnosis, or "getting lost" in a past life. Others have set their expectations of a particular way of experiencing past lives and feel disappointed when they experience it differently. I have come across patients who do not go into a past life simply because a lot is already going on in their current life at that particular moment and their mind is telling them to sort out things now rather than to look elsewhere. In such instances, their resistance to regression should be respected.

Comparative Healing

In the inner healing achievable through past life therapy, our epistemological assumptions are shifted to embrace the possibility that the *subtle world* (energy fields) can change the *physical world* (body) and not merely the reverse. While modern physicians may speak of mortality and morbidity, the regression therapist and the holistic physician think in terms of healing the *shadow self*[25] and growth of the soul.

In Medicine, the classic model of biological wound healing has three overlapping phases:

(1) *Inflammatory phase* in which bacteria and debris at the wound are removed and growth factors are secreted to cause the migration and division of cells involved in the next phase.

(2) *Proliferative phase* where there is proliferation of fibroblasts, production of collagen, new vessel formation, deposition of granulation tissue, re-epithelialization and wound contraction.

(3) *Remodeling phase* in which collagen is remodeled along tension lines along with removal of unwanted cells and increasing tensile strength of the wounds.

---

[25] The shadow, according to Jung, is the unconscious part of the personality that tends to be largely negative, instinctive and irrational, and prone to projection.

Fig. 25: Comparative Healing

	Wound Healing (Biological)	Past Life Healing (Holistic)
Phase 1	**Inflammatory** Inflammatory cell response and release of growth factors and cytokines	**Abreaction** Recall of traumatic event with cathartic response and release of pent-up emotions
Phase 2	**Proliferative** Increase in fibroblasts, angiogenesis, collagen deposition and granulation tissue	**Pattern Exploration** Increase in meaningful knowledge upon discovery of linking patterns leads to new interpretations of current lifetime
Phase 3	**Remodeling** Collagen re-aligned along tension lines allows the physical strength of the wound to increase	**Transformation** Past experience reframed allows insight into the hidden self and leads to change of behavior

In past life therapy, healing originates from the mind rather than the body and the process begins with an exploration of the mind-soul interaction. Likewise it goes through three overlapping phases but the parallels may seem subtle.

Phase (1): Abreaction

The patient identifies himself with a previous lifetime, during which he lives out the actual physical experience and the emotions of a traumatic past life situation. With close support from the therapist, there might be a flood of emotions including the release of fear, grief, pain and despair when the past life story is experienced fully in the body. During this phase the blocked energy is released with the old trauma. The release may appear frightening to an uninformed observer, but is nonetheless crucial for healing.

Phase (2): Search for Patterns

During this stage the patient emerges from his participatory role and takes on a witness position in order to observe the patterns of that past life. He is now able to observe and evaluate what he has been through and search for the existence of recurrent emotional patterns between past and current lifetimes. These patterns can be in the form of metaphors and symbolic images. Such patterns are crucial to regression therapy. The purpose of understanding patterns is to become aware that much of the patient's life is strongly predetermined by what he had done in other lifetimes. Identification of the pattern linking lifetimes leads to an enormous increase in the patient's conscious knowledge. The patient suddenly learns how to interpret and understand details of his present life in a new manner.

Phase (3): Transformation

As the spiritual self appreciates the parallels between events and emotions of the past life character and the current persona, the therapist gives support for releasing pent-up anger, denial and guilt. A commonly used intervention at this stage is that of *reframing*. It is the act of changing a patient's perspective and re-experiencing an event in a different light in order to change the meaning. As the meaning of an event changes, the patient's behavior and responses also change. When a situation is reframed the emotional impact is transformed. The intention behind the symptom is separated from the symptom itself. Any inappropriate behavioral pattern is reframed by the patient so that it is perceived to occur in a more useful context. Many physical illnesses, handicaps and relationships may also be reframed within a past life scenario to provide a meaningful perspective. The patient learns to differentiate between the object he sees and that which the object veils, and to contact the reality behind the veil. The patient's *Higher Mind* often helps to provide the insight. Change allows for constant regeneration and renewal. As the light of the soul pours forth to illuminate the brain, healing takes place.

The Death Point

In general, a lot of insight from any previous lifetime can be uncovered and expressed at the time of death. A person going through the death point often remembers quite vividly the experience and the memories about leaving the physical body. As a rule, the last conscious thought before the soul leaves the body sets an intention that is carried into the next lifetime. Upon death, the life force energy withdraws from the physical body and the soul enters a new world invisible to ordinary sight.

Following this the soul may be brought to the inter-life, a time of rest and refreshment after the lessons learned from the earth's school. This is part of the process of *integration*. The release of the soul out of the surroundings where it still feels painful and unhappy into an environment where he may possibly project love and warmth can help the patient to change and heal. Next the soul is gently led into another period during which it acquires a deeper understanding of the mystery of its own being. While it re-evaluates its progress in the unfolding of its divine attributes it is also presented with a panoramic view of its many incarnations on earth. Gradually the soul begins to grasp a vision of those special spiritual gifts which when developed enable it to contribute to wholesomeness. It then realizes that to acquire the necessary gifts, further learning through another physical body is required. At this stage it senses the need to reincarnate once more.

Besides setting patterns for another lifetime, death offers the opportunity for a review of the life just lived and makes reframing possible through an expanding of perspective.

Unlike in traditional Medicine where death is deemed to be a failure of treatment, regression therapists perceive death as a change of dimension. It is a transition from the physical body to the astral body and eventually to a soul plane form. Hypnotic techniques allow us to merge with our *Higher Self* at the moment of death and leave the karmic cycle once and for all.

The Reversal

Finally the regression process ends with bringing the patient back into ordinary consciousness. The patient emerging from a successful regression will have acquired a large volume of knowledge stemming from the scenes and events he has witnessed in his past life. Personally I am inclined to use positive affirmations and healing imagery before guiding the patient on his return to the here and now. While the outcomes of therapy can manifest anytime from days to months after the therapy, the healing effects are frequently dramatic and sometimes exceed expectations.

Sometimes a creative ability, such as an artistic skill, may emerge from a past life memory for which the patient could find no explanation. It is not uncommon to hear of patients feeling transformed in such a way that they are able to give and receive love and extend forgiveness to those who have wronged them. Some patients may discover that they no longer fear death. Having experienced and visualized it under regression, they may no longer view death as being the end of their life journey. Rather, it is seen as a change in scenery.

Conclusion

The theoretical model of regression therapy is not based on the natural sciences nor physical phenomena. Rather it is based on a structure of consciousness and requires our openness to all human experiences regardless of how odd they seem. The emphasis of the methodology is on pluralism, and three modalities of knowledge are involved – the sensory, the intellectual and the contemplative. Such pluralism is a reflection of postmodernism. It implies that a scientific approach to understanding the human psyche must involve multiple perspectives. It is expected that both the practitioner and his patients will experience a certain amount of awe and curiosity while remaining open to the mystery of the inner psyche.

Further Reading

Bennet, G., *The Wound and the Doctor: Healing, Technology and Power in Modern Medicine*, Secker & Warburg 1987 – This interesting book is written by a doctor who started his career as a surgeon and went on to become a psychotherapist and psychiatrist. He addresses the issue of why many doctors are unhappy with the work they do and many patients are unhappy about the care they receive, and how things could be better. He also dwells on the role of complementary therapies.

Churchill, R., *Regression Hypnotherapy – Transcripts of Transformation*, Transforming Press, 2002 – This book contains teaching material and full transcripts of current life regression sessions for a variety of conditions including phobias, grief, lack of confidence, sabotaging success, unhealthy relationships, abuse and fear of abandonment. It is an excellent guide for beginners as well as a useful reference for experienced therapists.

LaBay, M.L., *Past Life Regression: A Guide for Practitioners*, Trafford Publishing, 2004 – A light reading book on the practice of past life therapy that incorporates stories from the author's personal experience. The author blends hypnotherapy techniques with philosophy, intuition and reincarnation theory to catalyze growth and transformation in her clients.

Lawton, I., *The Wisdom of the Soul – Profound insights from life between lives*, Rational Spirituality Press, 2007 – This is a book that provides evidence to support a rational belief in reincarnation and the inter-life. It is based on the findings of a wide range of research from numerous regression subjects. The consistency of the underlying elements of the inter-life experience allows the subject of spirituality to be presented in a rational way.

Lawton, I., *The Big Book of the Soul*, Rational Spirituality Press, 2008 - The author develops the approach to spirituality based on evidence rather than faith. It touches on a wide range of topics including near-death experience, out-of-body phenomena, past life therapy and inter-life regression. It is good reading for those who want to examine spirituality in an objective manner.

Lucas, W.B., *Regression Therapy: A Handbook for Professionals, Vols I & II*, Book Solid Press, 1992 - The two volumes are a classic for regression therapists. It is a multi-author work on regression therapy compiled by a professional psychologist and Jungian analyst. Volume 1 focuses on past life therapy while Volume II touches on prenatal and birth experiences, childhood traumas and death.

McNiff, S., *Art Heals: How Creativity Cures the Soul*, Shambhala, 2004 - A book that explains the healing value of art, imagery and imagination. The author touches on issues like treating images as people for dialogue and on engaging images as angels. It is a book based largely on the author's own transformational journey from an artist to a therapist.

Tomlinson, A., *Healing the Eternal Soul*, From the Heart Press, 2012 - This is a definitive reference work in regression therapy. The author shares his valuable experience in detail and uses concrete case studies to illustrate his points and techniques. It is a captivating book and a must-have for all students of regression therapy.

Tomlinson, A., *Exploring the Eternal Soul*, From the Heart Press, 2012 - The author takes the reader beyond the death experience and gives a wide and comprehensive explanation of the inter-life. He puts the content into a structured way that is easy to follow and understand. This is a highly recommended book for those of us who want to understand our life choices and what happens after death.

Tomlinson, A. (ed.), *Transforming the Eternal Soul*, From the Heart Press, 2011 - Written as a follow-on from *Healing the Eternal Soul*, it is packed with illuminating case studies and specialized therapy techniques. The chapters include: empowering a client; working with difficult clients; spiritual inner child regression; clearing dark energy; crystal therapy in regression; spiritual emergency; and integrating therapy into a client's current life.

Woolger, R.J., *Healing Your Past Lives*, Sounds True Inc., 2004 - This short book provides a series of interesting case studies that illustrate the power of uncovering past lives in the healing process. It gives insight as to how current life symptoms could be related to past life dramas and frozen memories. It also provides the reader with the key to unlocking the mysteries and questions they struggle with in their current lives.

Woolger, R.J., *Other Lives, Other Selves – A Jungian Psychotherapist Discovers Past Lives*, Bantam Books, 1988. A fascinating book that presents original insights into the emerging psychology of reincarnation. The book draws on both Western science and Eastern spirituality and explains how past lives may form the basis of transformation and healing in our lives.

Regression Therapy Associations

International Board of Regression Therapy (IBRT) - This is an independent examining and certifying board for past life therapists, researchers and training programs. Its mission is to set professional standards for regression therapists and organizations. The website has a list of international accredited past life training organizations.
Website: http://www.ibrt.org

Spiritual Regression Therapy Association (SRTA) - This is an international association of regression therapists that respect the spiritual nature of the clients. Established by Andy Tomlinson, they are professionally trained by the Past Life Regression Academy to international standards and work to a code of ethics that respects the clients' welfare.
Website: http://www.spiritual-regression-therapy-association.com

European Association of Regression Therapy (EARTh) - This is an independent worldwide association with the objective of creating and maintaining an international standard in regression therapy and improve and enlarge its professional acceptance. Every summer it offers a series of workshops for ongoing professional development. The website has a list of international accredited regression therapy training organizations.
Website: http://www.earth-association.org

About the Author

Dr. Peter Mack is a medical graduate from the University of Singapore and specialized in General Surgery, holding Fellowships from the Royal College of Surgeons of Edinburgh, and the Royal College of Physicians and Surgeons of Glasgow. He obtained his PhD in Medical Science from Lund University, Sweden; MBA from the Business School of the National University of Singapore; Master in Health Economics from Curtin University; and Master in Medical Education from the University of Dundee. He serves as an adjunct associate professor at Duke's Graduate Medical School, NUS. He is a certified hypnotherapist with NGH, IMDHA and IACT and holds a Diploma from the Past Life Regression Academy. He is the author of *Healing Deep Hurt Within*, and a contributing author to *Transforming the Eternal Soul*.

To contact the author, email: dr.pmack@gmail.com

Other Books by the Author

Healing Deep Hurt Within – The transformational journey of a young patient undergoing regression therapy

This book is about the true story of an emotionally traumatized lady at the depths of despair, and how she is able to recover from her devastated state through intensive regression therapy with a hospital-based physician. She turned around in 18 days, and dramatically changed herself to move on in life. Upon recovery, she requested that her physician write up her story of transformation for the benefit of others.

"A book that touches my heart." – Dr. Rudy Phen, Physician

"I think this book is an excellent demonstration of how hypnosis and regression work can be used as a collaborative methodology, mixing well with conventional treatments, much more efficiently and effectively than just using psychotherapy or medical treatments alone. It is easy to read and hard to put down!" – Virginia Waldron, Regression Therapist

"It is one of the greatest books I have ever read about regression therapy and hypnosis. The way the author is trusting his client and himself is a very powerful mind opener for me. It is not only what he has written; the magic lies between the lines." – Sven Heck, Regression Therapist

www.ingramcontent.com/pod-product-compliance
Lightning Source LLC
Chambersburg PA
CBHW072000290426
44109CB00018B/2083